DID ADAM HAVE A BELLYBUTTON?

AND OTHER TOUGH QUESTIONS ABOUT THE BIBLE

by
KEN HAM

Master Books

First printing, February 2000
Fifth printing, February 2004

ISBN: 0-89051-283-3
Library of Congress Card Number: 99-069313

Printed in the United States of America

Text layout: Diane King
Cover Illustration: Bryan Miller, Miller Illustration
Cover Design: Janell Robertson

For information regarding author interviews, please contact the publicity department at (870) 438-5288.

Please visit our website for other great titles:
www.masterbooks.net

Table of Contents

Note: The question of whether Adam had a bellybutton
is answered on page 183.

THE BOOK OF GENESIS

Garden of Eden

The fall

The flood

CREATION EVANGELISM

Evolutionary Arguments

Fossil Record

THE STATE OF THE WORLD

Death & Disease

Racism

families & Schools

THE
BOOK
of
GENESIS

Q. *Are the creation accounts in Genesis 1 and 2 contradictory?*

A. First, we need to understand that Genesis 1 gives an order of creation that was chronological — days one, two, three, four, five, and six. But Genesis 2 is not meant to be a chronology. It's intended to provide the details of day six, especially the creation of man and woman. Chapter 2 is setting the scene for what happens in Genesis 3. Therefore, these aren't contradictory accounts but complementary.

For example, in Genesis 1:27 it states that God made male and female. In Genesis 2, we're given the details as to how God did this — by taking dust and making the man, and making a woman from his side.

Christ himself quoted from both these passages in Matthew 19 when giving the foundation for the doctrine of marriage. So, He certainly didn't believe that they were contradictory.

The answers from Genesis tell us that Genesis 2 is just a more detailed account of portions of Genesis 1.

Q. *Do men have one less rib than women because God took a rib from Adam's side to make Eve?*

A. Men and women have exactly the same number of ribs. But it's an important question, and not as silly as it might sound. Let me explain.

First, just because God took a rib from Adam to make Eve would not mean that all of Adam's male descendants would have one less rib. Remember, it's our genes that determine how many ribs a person will have.

For example, if I lost a finger in an accident, and then had more children, they would not have one less finger! This is because the blueprint for our bodies is in the genes, the DNA in our cells. So if we lose something like a rib or a finger, this in no way affects the genes which we pass on to our children.

Second, remember from your biology that ribs "regenerate." In other words, Adam would've had his missing rib back quite quickly.

A fascinating question, with an answer from Genesis!

Q. *How was Adam able to name all the animals on the sixth day of creation, and how was he later able to remember all of their names?*

A. First, we need to understand that just because we wouldn't have the brain power to come up with names for the many animals that God created, doesn't mean that Adam couldn't. You see, Adam had a perfect brain. We don't, because our brain has suffered from thousands of years of sin and the curse. Frankly, we're nowhere near as intelligent as Adam was.

Now think about this: our brain is considered to be the most complicated structure in the entire universe. It's far more complicated than the most advanced super computer we have today. And remember, it's man's brain that invents computers. When God first made Adam's brain with a perfect memory, it would be easy for Adam to name all the animals and to remember millions of pieces of information. If our own brain can make a computer to store information, then our all-powerful God can certainly make Adam's brain to do much more.

The answer's in Genesis — naming the animals and remembering their names was easy for Adam.

Q. *Was the Garden of Eden in the Middle East, where we find the Tigris and Euphrates Rivers?*

A. Well, I'm afraid I have to tell you that we have absolutely no idea where the Garden of Eden was located.

The Bible describes the Garden as being associated with four rivers that arise from one source. This description does not fit with the location of the Tigris and Euphrates Rivers today. Furthermore, this area of the Middle East is on top of thousands of feet of rocks containing billions of dead things.

Think about this: Since death came into the world after sin, we cannot have the Garden of Eden sitting on billions of dead bones showing evidence of diseases, pain, and suffering!

You see, we need to remember that the whole world was destroyed by the flood of Noah's day. The Garden of Eden would've also been destroyed. During the flood, the continents probably split apart forming a totally different-looking earth to that before the flood.

When Noah came out of the ark and into this new world, he would've used names he was familiar with, like Tigris and Euphrates, to name the rivers he saw.

Q. *Does the Bible tell us whether or not Adam and Eve could eat meat?*

A. In Genesis 1:30, we're told that God created a perfect world, and He instructed the beasts of the earth, the fowl of the air, and everything that creeps on the earth to eat every green herb for food. In other words, the animals originally were created to be vegetarian. Now what about Adam and Eve?

First, we need to know that the Bible teaches that there was no death or bloodshed until after Adam sinned. So man also was created to be vegetarian, but was told that he could eat meat after the flood. (That's found in Genesis 9.)

Once we have our answers from Genesis, we can understand why the world is full of death and suffering today. It's because of sin. Originally, man and animals were all vegetarian. The fact that many creatures are not vegetarian today is actually a reminder of Adam's rebellion — and our rebellion — against our Creator, and our need for a Savior.

Q. *Didn't the plants die when animals ate them in the Garden of Eden?*

A. When I make the claim that the Bible teaches there was no death before sin, I'm referring to the death and bloodshed of animals and humans.

When God originally made the animals, He created them to be vegetarian. It was only after the Fall that man was told that he could eat meat. However, if animals and man ate plants before sin, doesn't that mean that there was death because plants died?

Well, the Bible has the answer. It tells us that plants are not living in the same sense that animals are. The Hebrew word nephesh is used in Genesis for animals and man. This word signifies the "life principle" that animals — and man — have. But this word isn't used for plants. They don't have the "life principle" that animals have. Plants were given for food; they don't "die" in the animal sense.

The answers from Genesis tell us that there was no death, bloodshed, disease, or suffering before sin. All these things are a consequence of sin. That's why Christians can't believe in millions of years for the fossil record — it's a horrible record of death, disease, and suffering, which couldn't have happened in the Garden before Adam fell.

Q. *Was there disease before Adam sinned?*

A. I've found that the majority of Christians, and even most Christian leaders, have accepted the evolutionists' teaching of millions of years for the fossil record. In doing so, many haven't realized that they've also accepted horrible diseases before sin.

Let me explain. There's a special branch of science called paleopathology. This is the study of diseases in fossils. For instance, dinosaur bones that are supposedly millions of years old have been found to show evidence of arthritis, abscesses, and osteoarthritis. Evidence of cancer and other diseases have also been found in fossil bones.

So, if a Christian believes the fossil record was laid down millions of years before the first two people, then they've accepted that there were all sorts of horrible diseases in this world before sin. How could God have described such a world as VERY GOOD?

By the way, many of the diseases found in the fossil bones are the same sorts of diseases that also affect humans.

No — our answers in Genesis make it clear that there were NO diseases before sin. This is another reason why Christians cannot believe in millions of years to form the fossil record.

Q. *Was the forbidden fruit that Adam ate in the Garden an apple?*

A. Frankly, no. What this fruit from the "tree of the knowledge of good and evil" was is anyone's guess. But we do know this: there was a literal tree, a literal temptation of Adam and Eve, and a literal fruit that they ate. Therefore, this was a literal rebellion against our Holy God.

As a result of this literal event, sin and death came into the world. This is the reason that mankind needs a Savior, because we all, in Adam, rebel against our Creator. In our children's book, A is for Adam, we pictured the forbidden fruit as looking something like a hand grenade. We were trying to make the point that Adam's action had a catastrophic result!

It's important for Christians to understand that if this event of the forbidden fruit was not history, then the Fall itself would not be literal. This would also mean that Christ's death on the cross would be meaningless.

Even though we don't know what the fruit was, we do know that it's so important to take Genesis as written. The basis of the whole gospel message, which starts in Genesis 3:15, is dependent on the Fall being real history.

Q. *Why did Adam get the blame when Eve was the one who took the first bite of the forbidden fruit?*

A. Even Paul, in both Romans and Corinthians, declared that it was Adam's sin that brought the judgment of death. So, if Adam received the blame, he must've been responsible. But why?

When you read Genesis, you find that it was Adam who was given the specific instruction not to eat the fruit of the tree. You see, Adam was created first, and God had ordained that he was to be the head of his family. He then gave Adam instruction as to what was expected of him. Adam, of course, would've told Eve, because she was really under his headship. Therefore, when Eve took the fruit, Adam shouldn't have joined her. He should've gone directly to God and asked Him for a solution. Instead, he joined his wife and brought sin and death into the world. You know, this is a lesson we need to learn today about men taking the leadership role in their families.

Today, many men are not the heads of their homes, which has led to many family problems. If husbands would get their answers from Genesis, they'd know that theirs is to be a headship role, and they're responsible for the rules God has given families.

THE FALL - 21

Q. *What are the effects of the fall of Adam?*

A. The apostle Paul, in Romans, describes this present creation as a groaning one. And it certainly is! Look around! You see people dying — animals dying. There are deadly diseases. The earth is filled with violence. In reality, this is not such a beautiful place!

However, Genesis has the explanation as to why we're in this sorry state. When Adam sinned — everything changed. God had to judge sin with death. From that time on, the whole of creation was affected. Everything started to run down. No longer did God uphold the creation in a perfect state.

But Christians who accept the idea of millions of years of earth's history are really denying that Adam's fall affected anything. You see, if the death and struggle we see in today's world has gone on for millions of years — then what change did sin bring? Nothing is different, then.

So what then did Paul mean when he stated that the whole of creation is travailing in pain? To accept millions of years is to deny the horrible affects of the Fall, as given by our answers in Genesis.

Q. *Why was it so necessary for Christ to die and shed His blood for us to be saved?*

A. Well, the Book of Hebrews tells us that without the shedding of blood there's no remission of sins. When you think about it, when Adam, the representative head of the entire human race, rebelled against his Holy Creator, he forfeited his right to live. God rightfully placed on Adam — and all his descendants — the judgment of death.

But God wants each of us to spend eternity with Him. So how can this be done? Well, since the first representative head brought sin and death into the world, the human race would need a new representative to pay the penalty for sin. But the one to pay this penalty couldn't be a sinner like us — it would have to be someone perfect.

Well, God had a wonderful solution. The Lord Jesus Christ, the Son of God, became a man — a perfect man — who suffered the penalty for sin . . . and shed His blood. God the Father raised Him from the dead as proof that this sacrifice was accepted.

Christ, who is also called the last Adam, became our new representative head so that all who trust in Him can be saved.

Why did Jesus shed His blood? The answer's in Genesis — death was the penalty for sin.

Q. *Is the meaning of clothing connected to the Book of Genesis?*

A. In Genesis 3:21, we're told that God made the first clothes for the first two people. Because Adam and Eve had sinned, they also saw their nakedness; God then killed animals to give them coats of skins.

Actually, this sad event is also a beautiful picture of what was to come. The first blood sacrifice in Genesis as a covering for sin was a picture of what Christ, the Lamb of God, was going to do on the cross of Calvary.

God gave Adam and Eve clothes because of sin. Now sin distorts nakedness — in fact, it distorts everything. Since God made clothes because of sin, it means that there's a moral basis for clothing. When you think about it, it's only the Christian who has a real basis for insisting on wearing clothes and that there are standards of how we should dress.

As societies reject their answers from Genesis, people will abandon Christian doctrines such as wearing clothes. We see that more and more people build their thinking on evolutionary ideas instead of the authority of the Word of God.

Q. *When was the first death?*

A. I know for sure that the first death to occur was that of an animal, about 6,000 years ago. The animal was probably a lamb.

Now, how can I be so sure about this? Well, our answers in Genesis state that when Adam sinned, God killed an animal to obtain coats of skins for Adam and Eve. This was the first blood sacrifice as a covering for their sin. In fact, this was really a picture of the gospel.

Remember, Hebrews teaches us that without the shedding of blood, there can be no remission of sins. Personally, I think the animal God killed probably was a lamb — it was a picture of what was to come in Jesus Christ — the Lamb of God who taketh away the sin of the world.

However, Christians who believe that the fossil record is millions of years old, also accept that death and bloodshed existed before Adam sinned. Thus, the shedding of blood would have nothing to do with sin! Belief in millions of years of death and bloodshed destroys the foundations of the gospel message.

Q. *Can we know for sure who Cain married?*

A. Well, to answer this question, let's consider the following passages of Scripture:

First Corinthians 15:45 states that "The first man Adam was made a living soul."

Genesis 3:20 tells us that Eve "was the mother of all the living."

And in Acts 17 we read that all people are of "one blood."

Thus, the Bible makes it clear that all people are related because they are descendants of one man and one woman.

Now Genesis 5:4 tells us that Adam and Eve had sons and daughters. This means that ORIGINALLY, brothers, like Cain, MUST HAVE married sisters. Keep in mind that the law against close relatives marrying didn't come into being until the time of Moses.

Because of the effects of sin, mistakes have added up in the genes of humans so that today, deformities could result from close relatives marrying. Adam and Eve's children would have had relatively few mistakes in the genes compared to today. So, provided it was one man for one woman for life — there would not have been a problem at all for Cain to marry his sister!

Q: *Was Noah's flood a local or a global catastrophe?*

A. None of us were there to see Noah's flood. So, the only way we can know for sure if this event really occurred, and if it was a global or local event, is if an eyewitness recorded what happened.

Now we have an eyewitness who had the events of history recorded so we can be 100 percent sure of what happened. The God of history moved men by His Spirit to write His Word.

In God's Word, we read that Noah's flood was a REAL event in history. Not only that, we're told that the waters of the flood covered "ALL" the high hills under ALL of heaven. This double "ALL," plus the rest of what's recorded in Genesis 7, make it obvious it was a GLO-BAL event.

The reason some Christians don't believe God's Word, is because they listen to the words of fallible men who believe in millions of years of earth history — instead of the very clear ANSWERS from the infallible Creator.

Q. Why do some Christians insist that Noah's flood was a local event?

A. When you read the account of the flood in Genesis, the language is emphatic that this was a global-destroying flood, where the highest hills under the whole of heaven were covered.

Also, a number of passages in the Bible compare the judgment in Noah's day with that of the coming judgment by fire — both judgments are obviously global ones.

So, why do some Christians insist that Noah's flood was a local event? The main reason is because they've accepted the evolutionists' teaching that the fossil record is millions of years old. They recognize that a global flood would destroy such a record and lay down a new one. Thus, they relegate Noah's flood to just a local event in their attempt to cling to their belief in millions of years.

Not only does this compromise position do violence to the Scriptures, but it allows for the death, disease, bloodshed, violence, and suffering in the fossil record to occur before Adam's sin. This is OPPOSITE to what Genesis teaches. Death came AFTER sin.

Q. *How did Noah collect all the different kinds of land animals that were needed to go on the ark?*

A. My answer comes from Genesis 6:19-20: "And of every living thing of all flesh, two of every sort shalt thou bring into the ark, to keep them alive with thee; they shall be male and female. Of fowls after their kind, and of cattle after their kind, of every creeping thing of the earth after his kind, two of every sort shall come unto thee, to keep them alive."

God's Word tells us that Noah didn't have to go out and collect the animals. God sent them TO Noah.

I believe that God would have chosen the animals that had the best collection of genes to enable them to reproduce and survive in the world after the flood.

You know, when we think about the flood of Noah's day, we can never separate the supernatural element from all of this. The infinite Creator God was in total control of all that happened.

Q. *How did Noah deal with the animal dung of 16,000 animals on the ark?*

A. Skeptics often mock those of us who believe in the account of Noah's ark by claiming that Noah would've been buried deep in animal droppings.

One of our research scientists set out to see what he could find concerning the farming of animals and waste management. He concluded that Noah would've had no trouble dealing with waste.

By the way, animal husbandry is a real science. Our researcher found for instance that in Norwegian barns, the semi-solid excrement from cattle accumulates in storage pits designed to drain the liquid fraction away through openings. In other places in the world, straw is used to soak up liquid and the excrement is allowed to accumulate as a bed the animals live on!

There are also many inventive techniques such as slatted floors, sloped self-cleaning floors, and so on, that easily remove waste from situations where many animals are enclosed together.

Noah certainly had the ability to use such techniques and probably invent better ones. Even from today's world we can get ANSWERS to what seem to be problems with the Noah's ark account.

Q. *Is it true that Noah only took two of each kind of land animal on board the ark?*

A. No it certainly isn't. Let's read God's Word from Genesis 7:2: "Of every clean beast thou shalt take to thee by sevens, the male and his female: and of beasts that are not clean by two, the male and his female."

Thus, God's Word informs us that Noah actually took two of each of the unclean animals, and seven of each of the clean.

Now why was this necessary? I believe there are two reasons. First of all, after the flood in Genesis 8 we read that Noah took one of every clean beast and fowl and offered them as a sacrifice to the Lord. If there were only two each of these, they would've become extinct very quickly!

Second, the clean animals are those mostly associated with man for food and clothing. It would make sense that God would have Noah take more of these on board to the new world. By the way, there was plenty of room on this massive ark for all these animals.

It's SO important that we read God's Word carefully so we can have ANSWERS!

Q. *How did Noah fit all the animals on the ark?*

A. Over the years, especially on talk show programs, I've found that when people claim Noah didn't have room for all the animals on the ark, they've never figured out how many animals were needed on the ark.

Creation scientists have done some very careful calculations and found that Noah could not only have had representatives of all the land animals on board — but plenty of room to spare!

Now Noah didn't need to take all the SPECIES of land animals on board — just representatives of the KINDS. In other words, he didn't need all the varieties of dogs — just two dogs that would give rise to numerous species in the new world after the flood. Calculations show that probably only around 16,000 animals were needed on board the ark.

Without even considering the use of tiering for the animal enclosures, but giving the animals plenty of room, less than one-half of the ark would've been used up.

There are ANSWERS when one is prepared to research carefully!

Q. *Would dinosaurs have been on Noah's ark?*

A. Well, the Bible makes it clear in Genesis 6 that representatives of ALL the KINDS of land animals were on board Noah's ark. It's interesting to note that the list of animals given in Genesis 6 is the same list recorded in Genesis 1 concerning the KINDS of animals God created.

Because dinosaurs were land animals, they must've been included in the groups of animals God created. Therefore, I see no reason whatsoever to claim they weren't on the ark.

Now some people think dinosaurs were too big to fit on the ark. Actually, the average size of a dinosaur, from the skeletons that've been found, was about the size of a sheep. You see, only a few were large — probably because they were old. Personally, I think God sent "teenagers" on the ark rather than senior citizens!

Really, it's because people have been influenced by evolution that they think dinosaurs weren't on the ark. We need to get our ANSWERS from the Bible — not evolutionists!

Q. *Were there fish on board Noah's ark?*

A. When you read Genesis 6, you find that God's intention was to destroy all life on the land. In other words, people, and all the creatures that breathed air through nostrils (except for those on the ark), were to be destroyed.

Noah did not have to build a large aquarium on board the ark — in a sense, he sailed on top of one!

However, many of the aquatic creatures did die — although enough of them survived to repopulate the oceans, rivers, and lakes after the flood.

Many people, though, ask how freshwater fish would survive the flood's salty waters. Actually, we have to remember that the fish we have today are descendants of fish that lived at the time of the flood around 4,500 years ago. This means there has been a great deal of "natural selection" going on since the flood. Thus, fish today might not have all the information in their genes to enable them survive such a flood — but their ancestors many generations ago would have. This is natural selection "creation style."

It's exciting to know the ANSWERS that help us defend God's Word.

Q: *How did Noah fit all the thousands of species of animals that now live on earth on board the ark?*

A. First of all, Noah didn't take all the SPECIES of animals on the ark — just the KINDS. For instance, Noah didn't need the African elephant, the mammoth, and the stegodon on the ark. He just needed TWO elephants. After the flood, as the elephants spread out over the earth, different varieties resulted from the tremendous amount of information God put in the genes of these creatures.

Thus, Noah didn't need anywhere near the number of animals we think he did. Calculations indicate that he probably only had about 16,000 animals. There was plenty of room!

Secondly, many people think most land animals were large, like elephants, giraffes, and so on. However, only 11 percent of land animals are larger than a sheep. So, the average size of an animal that was on board the ark was MUCH smaller than that of a sheep.

When we research carefully, we find ANSWERS to show Noah's ark had plenty of room for the land animals.

Q. *Did the insects need to be on the ark in order to survive Noah's flood?*

A. Personally, I don't believe insects had to be on board. You see, I don't believe they're classified in the Bible as having the "breath of life" as vertebrates are. Thus, I don't believe two of every kind of insect had to board the ark.

Well if insects didn't have to be on the ark, how would they have survived a global flood?

First of all, some insects would obviously be on the ark — they would be carried in by other animals, and in the food and other materials carried on board.

However, I believe most insects survived outside the ark. When the flood occurred, we need to realize that there would've been massive quantities of plants, including large trees, floating on the surface of the waters. A lot of insects could have easily survived on such floating log mats.

As well as adult forms, insects could have survived as eggs, larvae, and pupae. I have no doubt all these forms could survive in various ways during the flood considering all the debris there would have been in the water.

Q. *How did the plants survive the global flood of Noah's day?*

A. I think there are at least four ways in which plants made it through the flood.

First of all, Noah would've taken grain and other seeds on board the ark. I think he would've particularly selected seeds of plants that would produce food for his family after the flood.

Second, many seeds would've floated on the water. Also, when a flood rips up vegetation, seeds that aren't ripe may stay attached to the plants (including trees) that would float.

Third, even though some seeds would sink, this wouldn't necessarily stop them from germinating once the flood waters ran off the land. I once saw a dam that was drained, and within a short period of time, all sorts of plants were germinating from seeds that had been in the mud at the bottom, probably for many years.

Fourth, many plants would've floated, and then taken root in the ground once the waters had abated. There are many plants today that we can reproduce vegetatively, without using seeds.

Yes — there are simple answers to questions surrounding the flood of Noah.

Q. *How did Noah and his family feed all the animals on the ark for a whole year?*

A. This certainly sounds like an impossible task, doesn't it? Now some creationists believe God may have supernaturally intensified an animal's ability to hibernate. This would have greatly reduced their body functions, thus requiring only minimal attention.

However, I don't even think this was necessary. One research scientist made a detailed study of factory farming in today's world. There are many instances today where farmers use quite ingenious methods to raise large numbers of animals. Also, inventions such as self-feeding devices can make a tremendous difference in the amount of time needed to feed animals.

Most of us tend to think of Noah as much less advanced than we are. Actually, the opposite would be true. We've had 4,500 more years of the effects of sin and the Curse on our brains. I'm convinced Noah would have had the intelligence necessary to devise methods of feeding and caring that would put today's farmers to shame.

If farmers today have methods that could easily allow eight people to look after 16,000 animals — I've no doubt Noah could do much more!

Q. If the whole earth was covered during Noah's flood, where did all the water come from?

A. In Genesis 7, the Bible records two major events that caused the water to cover the earth. First of all, we're told that the "fountains of the great deep" were opened. Presumably, vast quantities of subterraneous waters burst out of the ground. Actually, even in today's earth, there are massive amounts of water under the ground. Before the flood, there was probably even much more water stored in the earth.

The second event was when the windows of heaven were opened. This produced rain on the earth for 40 days and 40 nights. There must've been much more water vapor in the atmosphere before the flood, because if all the water vapor in our present atmosphere fell as rain, the ground would be covered to an average depth of less than two inches.

In addition to these two major events that poured massive amounts of water onto the earth, earthquakes, volcanic explosions, and tidal waves probably occurred all over the globe.

What a judgment it was on the wickedness of man!

Q. *Was there enough water to cover the earth's surface?*

A. When people say there wasn't enough water, and therefore Noah's flood couldn't have happened as the Bible states — they're making some invalid assumptions.

For instance, they're assuming that the mountains that exist today also existed at the time of the flood. However, this is not true. Did you know there are marine fossils on the top of Mount Everest? Actually, as you look at the mountain ranges on the earth, it's obvious they were uplifted at some time.

If you were to flatten out the mountains and the deep ocean basins, there would actually be enough water on the earth to cover it to a depth of nearly two miles.

I believe that the way God ended the flood was to raise up the mountains and lower the ocean basins. This caused the water to run off the earth, to where it is today.

In fact, 70 percent of the earth is still covered by the waters of the flood — what a sober reminder of God's judgment on a rebellious world!

Q. *How was the flood's rainbow significant?*

A. Some Christians miss a very important point here. You see, there are those in the Church who believe that Noah's flood was just a local event — not a global catastrophe.

However, God gave the covenant of the rainbow as a sign He would never again flood the earth as He did in Noah's day. Now consider this: we've seen lots of floods since this time. Every year, we see lots of news coverage of local floods in different parts of the world.

Now if Noah's flood was just a local event, then this means God did not keep His promise! But God AL-WAYS keeps His promises — therefore, Noah's flood couldn't have been just a local event. No, it was a global-destroying cataclysmic event — just as described in the Bible.

Every time we see a rainbow, we should be reminded of the global flood of Noah's day, and the fact that there will be another global judgment in the future — but next time it'll be by fire.

Q. *How is the scoffing of people today at the idea of believing in the global flood of Noah's day a "sign of our times"?*

A. In 2 Peter 3 we read the following:

Knowing this first, that there shall come in the last days scoffers, walking after their own lusts, And saying, Where is the promise of his coming? . . . For this they willingly are ignorant of, that by the word of God the heavens were of old, and the earth standing out of the water and in the water: Whereby the world that then was, being overflowed with water, perished.

Here Peter is telling us that a sign of the last days is that people will scoff at those who believe Jesus is coming again. As part of this scoffing they'll also reject the fact that God created and that He judged the world with a global flood.

How true this is of today's world! The majority of scientists scoff at those of us who believe in creation and the flood. Really, they aren't just scoffing at what we believe — they are scoffing at God's Word — just as most did in Noah's day. Yes, it's a sign of the times.

Q. *If there really was a global flood in Noah's day, as Genesis records — what evidence would we expect to find?*

A. One of my favorite sayings in answer to that question goes like this: If Noah's flood really happened, you would expect to find billions of dead things buried in rock layers, laid down by water all over the earth.

Now what do we find? Actually, we do find billions of dead things buried in rock layers, laid down by water all over the earth.

Of course, the evolutionists say, "But there's no evidence for a global flood — where's the evidence? After all," they say, "all we find is billions of dead things, buried in rock layers, laid down by water all over the earth."

I believe that most of the fossil record IS the evidence of Noah's flood. Of course, this evidence we see only exists in the present — therefore, one has to interpret what the fossil record really means. The more scientists have looked at it, the more it's obvious that it fits with catastrophism — not slow processes over millions of years.

The reason many scientists don't want to believe in a global flood is because it means the Bible is true!

Q. *Did Noah's ark really land on Mount Ararat?*

A. Actually, the Bible states that the ark landed on the MOUNTAINS of Ararat. In other words, we don't know which mountain was its resting place.

I've had lots of people over the years say that if we could only find Noah's ark, then we could convince people the Bible's true. But you know what? Even though it would be a great find, I personally don't believe this would convince many people to believe the Bible.

I'm reminded of a professor who once said to me after I spoke at a secular college, "I don't care if they do find a big boat on the top of Mount Ararat and drag it down Main Street — I still won't believe it's Noah's ark."

At another meeting, a man said to me, "Who's to say some priests didn't build a big boat on Mount Ararat because they wanted people to believe the story in the Bible?"

We need to be reminded that, as the Bible says, "The heart is deceitful above all things and desperately wicked." Because we are sinners, our nature is to want to reject the truth — regardless of the evidence.

Q. *How is Noah's ark a picture of Christ and salvation?*

A. Many people think of Noah's ark as just an enormous boat that God used to save land animals and Noah's family. But there is much more to learn from this account than the preserving of animals and eight people.

To be saved from the global flood that was about to destroy the earth, Noah and his family had to go through the doorway of the ark to be saved. I'm sure Noah must've been preaching right up until the time he went into the ark.

I could imagine him saying, "Come into the ark to be saved — there's plenty of room. You must come through this doorway to be saved." Sadly, only Noah's family was saved. When you think about it, this is a picture of salvation of which the ark is a type — it represents Jesus Christ.

Jesus said, "I am the door." To be saved, a person must go through the doorway — the Lord Jesus Christ. Just as there was only ONE way to be saved from the flood — there is only ONE way to be saved from the judgment to come — Jesus is the only WAY to heaven.

Q. *What does Noah's time have to do with the second coming of Christ?*

A. Well, Jesus Christ himself spoke of the days of Noah in relation to His coming again. Let's read Matthew 24:37–39: *But as the days of Noe were, so shall also the coming of the Son of man be. For as in the days that were before the flood they were eating and drinking, marrying and giving in marriage, until the day that Noe entered into the ark, And knew not until the flood came, and took them all away; so shall also the coming of the Son of man be.*

Jesus obviously believed the account given in Genesis.

Also, we know that at the time of the Second Coming, there will be a final judgment. This again attests to the fact that Noah's flood must've been a global judgment, because the coming judgment will be global also.

And finally, the rebellion in the days of Noah fits the description of the rebellion we see today. This should be a warning to all of us that the Second Coming is imminent. Are you ready to meet your Creator when He comes again?

Q: *What does the planet Mars have to do with Noah's flood?*

A. It was fascinating to read the newspaper reports concerning the Pathfinder mission which landed a spacecraft on Mars. Scientists have been interested in the canyons they've seen on Mars. In fact, they believe these canyons were formed by the action of water.

In one of the newspapers, the reporter stated that scientists believed a "flood of biblical proportions" occurred on Mars.

I had to smile when I read this. You see, the majority of scientists don't believe a flood of biblical proportions occurred on earth — which is mostly covered by water. Yet these same scientists believe there was a massive flood on Mars — which has no water!

Now, why is this? Personally, I believe scientists would be only too happy to have a global flood on earth like the Bible describes — except for this: it would mean that the Bible is true, that God does judge sin, and that every person must acknowledge their sinful state and kneel before their Creator! This is the real reason many people don't want to believe the account of Noah's flood.

Q. *Why don't all scientists believe in Noah's flood?*

A. This is actually a very important question. You know, after I've given lectures in schools and colleges, I often get this same question. You see, once the students have heard that the layers of the Grand Canyon can be explained by the flood — not slow processes, and once they've been told that fossils can form quickly, and once they've been shown the evidence that coal deposits didn't form in swamps over millions of years, but were formed from plant material dumped by lots of water — then these students usually ask, "If this is all true — why don't our teachers and all scientists believe this?"

The answer can be found in the Bible in 2 Peter 3:5. Concerning people rejecting the belief in creation and the flood, Peter tells us that people are willingly ignorant — which means they deliberately reject or REFUSE to believe this. In other words — it has nothing to do with the evidence — they don't want to believe. It's because of our sin nature — we are in rebellion against our Creator.

Q. *How did Noah build such an enormous ship?*

A. You know, skeptics often mock the idea that a man called Noah could build a massive ark 4,500 years ago. They claim that ships the size of the ark couldn't be built until the 19th century.

However, as is usual in today's world, this assumes that people hundreds or thousands of years ago were nowhere near as advanced as we are today. In fact, because of evolutionary thinking there appears to be an assumption that peoples of long ago were little more than savages.

However, archaeological discoveries keep proving the exact opposite — which of course fits with the biblical account of origins — that the first man was highly intelligent to start with.

Researchers have found that the Chinese — at the time of Marco Polo — built enormous seagoing junks. In the 15th century, the Chinese built junks that approached the size of the ark. There's also evidence that the ancient Greeks had a ship that could carry about 4,000 tons of cargo.

The point is, Noah, with his sons, could've had technology we don't even know about today to easily build this boat.

Q. *Could a man who could build a ship the size of the ark be primitive?*

A. You know, many people think that Noah couldn't have built the ark as described in the Bible. After all, Noah didn't have all the electric tools we have today. And how would he ever design the ark without computers?

Actually, we don't know what kind of technology Noah had. In fact, it's very possible he had better technology than we have today.

You see, because of the influence of evolutionary teaching, most people tend to think that people in past generations were not as good or intelligent as we are today. They think we're obviously advanced, because we have jet planes and computers!

However, the Bible makes it plain that the first man, Adam, was highly intelligent. His descendants went out and built cities and made musical instruments. Sadly, because of sin and the Curse, everything has been running down for 6,000 years. I'm sure our brain today is nowhere near as good as Adam's was. I'm also sure Noah was extremely intelligent. We'd probably be amazed at the methods he used to build the ark.

No — Noah was not primitive. In fact, if Noah was here today, he would probably call us primitive!

Q. *Was Noah a great man of God?*

A. He certainly was. You know, I've often thought about Noah compared to people today. You see, God's Word tells us that Noah's flood occurred about 4,500 years ago. If this event really happened, we'd expect to find evidence of this all over the earth.

And we do! We find billions of fossils buried in layers of rock that were deposited by water. The evidence for the flood is overwhelming!

You know — sadly, the majority of people today, including many who claim to be Christians, don't believe Noah's flood happened as the Bible records — yet the evidence in the fossil record is staring them right in the face!

Noah didn't have any evidence like this to go on. He just had to trust the Word of God that this event really was going to happen.

What a different place this world would be if people, including Christians, would believe God's Word just as Noah did. One of my favorite verses in the Bible is Psalm 119:160: *Thy word is true from the beginning.*

Q. *What is the truth about the curse of Ham?*

A. Over the years, I've often listened to people talk about the supposed curse of Ham. Sadly, I've also heard some people, including some Christian leaders, claim that this curse resulted in the black-skinned people being formed. Frankly, this is nonsense.

The Bible makes it clear in Genesis 9 that it was Ham's youngest son Canaan who was cursed. In fact, Ham had four sons, and there was no curse placed on his other three sons.

I believe that what was happening here was that Noah recognized that Canaan's nature was very much like his father Ham — only worse. Just as Ham brought disrespect to Noah, so Canaan would also bring disrespect to his father Ham. This is exactly what happened.

As you read the Bible, you find that Canaan's descendants were the evil Canaanites and the people of Sodom and Gomorrah. What Noah said about Canaan was shown to be true.

There's also a warning here for fathers. Ham's rebellious nature certainly influenced the next generation — and sadly, as usually happens, this rebellion became much worse, generation after generation.

Q. *After Noah's ark, how did kangaroos ever get to Australia?*

A. Well, the simplest answer is that they hopped!

However, some would think they'd have to have an enormous hop to get across the ocean to Australia. But I believe there's actually a simple solution to this.

Scientists have found lots of evidence that around one-third of the earth's surface has been covered by ice. There's evidence, for example, that large glaciers once carved the Great Lakes in North America.

Creationists believe that this "ice age" occurred sometime after the flood — because of the flood. With warm water, cool land, and ash in the atmosphere blocking out sunlight at the end of the flood, there would be a lot of evaporation. The precipitation would come in the form of ice and snow.

The build-up of ice and snow would lower oceans by around 600 feet — forming land bridges all over the earth. This would enable animals like kangaroos to migrate to different parts of the earth, and then eventually the ice would have receded to where it is today.

Q. *What are cavemen and where did they come from?*

A. I have a very simple definition of cavemen: cavemen are men that live in caves!

Because of the influence of evolutionary ideas, which have popularized Neanderthal man as a less-than-human caveman, most people think cavemen have something to do with evolution. However, there are people in today's world who live in caves.

Now the Bible tells us that Noah lived in a tent — so I don't think he was caveman. However, when Noah's descendants started spreading out over the earth after the Tower of Babel — some people would've used caves for shelter. This doesn't mean they were primitive — they just used the best shelter they could find before most of them would eventually build homes.

In Australia there is an interesting opal mining town where it's very hot. Some of the people live in caves under the ground — real live cavemen . . . and with TV sets! Just because people live in caves doesn't mean they are primitive!

We need to get rid of evolutionary ideas about man's origin, and get our ANSWERS from the Bible, beginning with Genesis.

Q. How could Noah's flood have caused an "ice age"?

A. Scientists know that about one-third of the earth's surface was once covered by ice. There's a lot of evidence consistent with glaciers forming lakes and so on. Evolutionists postulate there were a series of ice ages over hundreds and millions of years. However, they have a big problem — using computer models, they can't get an ice age to work!

You see, you can't have an earth getting colder and colder — it would freeze over!

Now creationists believe in one ice age after the flood — and the computer models WORK. At the end of the flood, because of volcanic action and continental movement, the oceans would have been warm and the land cool. Ash in the atmosphere would have blocked out sunlight, also causing a cooling effect. Therefore, lots of water would have evaporated, and then precipitated in the form of ice and snow — causing an ICE AGE.

As things started to settle down, the ice would have begun to melt back to where it is today. The ice age can only be explained by the answers in Genesis!

Q. *Did Noah eat meat, and why is this important?*

A. Personally, I think Noah was a vegetarian until after the flood. You see, in Genesis 1:29–30, God told Adam and Eve — and the animals — that they were to be vegetarians.

This fits with the fact that there was no death, bloodshed, or disease before sin.

Now after Adam sinned, everything changed. I suspect some animals became carnivorous. Maybe even some of the people who rebelled against God started eating animals. We don't know, of course. However, I believe Noah remained a vegetarian, because he was a man who loved and obeyed God. I don't believe Noah would have rebelled against God's laws.

But in Genesis 9:3, after the flood, God told Noah that just as He gave the plants to be eaten originally, now they could eat meat. This means Noah may have started eating meat from this time on.

This is an important point, because it reminds us that there was no death of animals or people before sin. Thus, a person cannot believe in fossils forming over millions of years before sin.

Q. *How did animals change after Noah's flood?*

A. First of all, think back to the world before sin. It must've been a beautiful place — no death or disease. Adam and Eve wouldn't have been frightened of the animals — and the animals wouldn't have feared them. They were all vegetarian. As the Bible states — everything was very good.

Because of sin, though, things started to change. By the time of Noah's flood, people had rebelled against God — lots of changes were now occurring.

However, the animals must not have feared man as they do today, because the representatives of each kind went on board the ark.

At the end of the flood, in Genesis 9:2, we read:

> *And the fear of you and the dread of you shall be upon every beast of the earth, and upon every fowl of the air, upon all that moveth upon the earth, and upon all the fishes of the sea; into your hand are they delivered.*

God changed the behavior of the animals. From now on they would fear man. Sin really has disrupted this once-perfect world. What a sobering reminder.

Q. *Did dinosaurs once live in the Middle East?*

A. Actually, did you know that representatives of EVERY KIND of animal that God created once lived in the Middle East? This would have included kangaroos, koalas, wombats, bears, and so on.

How do I know this? Well, the Bible tells us that a man called Noah built an ark to save him, his family, and representatives of all the kinds of land animals during the global flood God sent as a judgment.

And where did this ark land after the flood? In the mountains of Ararat — the land known today as the Middle East.

Some people, though, think that dinosaurs weren't on board the ark. However, the Bible tells us that God sent representatives of ALL the kinds of land animals — which must have included dinosaurs.

By the way — most dinosaurs were small anyway — and even big ones were once small. However, Noah's ark was so big, there was room for large adult dinosaurs, if necessary.

Getting your answers from Genesis certainly makes you think differently about such things doesn't it?

Q. *Are there references to a global flood in the histories of other peoples?*

A. Actually, the Hawaiians, Eskimoes, American Indians, Australian Aborigines — in fact, most cultures in the world — have stories from their ancestors that sound like the event of Noah's flood recorded in Genesis.

Because I'm from Australia, I've collected some of the dreamtime legends told by the Aborigines before they ever met missionaries. One legend goes something like this:

> Ngadja, the supreme being, looked down
> on the man he had made. He was angry
> with Gajara for the way he'd treated
> Dumbi the winking owl. So he warned
> Gajara he was going to send a flood —
> and he was to build a raft and put on it
> the cockatoo and kangaroo — and
> ground meal for food. The raft landed on
> a mountain — and God put a rainbow in
> the sky to tell them what the weather
> would be like.

You know why the Aborigines have stories like this? They were handed down from Noah! Sadly, the stories have changed — but the real record is in the Bible. What a point of contact this can be to witness to the Aborigines.

Q. *Is it true that most cultures around the world have flood legends similar to the account in Genesis?*

A. Flood legends are found in cultures throughout the world. The Fijians, Hawaiians, Eskimos, American Indians, and Australian Aborigines — all have such accounts. There's no doubt that these legends have been handed down for generations — they had them long before they ever met missionaries who brought the Bible to them.

And it's interesting to note the similarities in these accounts: a flood that covered the earth — a boat built by a man to save people and animals — it landed on a mountain, and so on. Often, three sons are mentioned, and the name of their father is very similar to Noah.

The Australian Aborigines even have a rainbow in the sky at the end of the flood.

Now why do these cultures all have such similar accounts? These stories have been handed down since the time of Noah. Over the years they have changed — but the same basic elements are still there.

Of course, the original and true account has been handed down in written form in the Bible. This attests to the fact that all these people are descendants of Noah — we are all one race!

Q. What is important about the fact that cultures throughout the world have legends that sound like Genesis 1–11?

A. I recall the time a missionary to the Australian Aborigines attended one of our seminars.
Because I knew that cultures all over the world had flood legends similar to the historical account in Genesis, I asked him if the Aborigines had any such stories. I explained to him that the reasons these stories abound all over the world is that they were handed down from the time of Noah, even though they were changed somewhat. The real record, of course, is in the Bible. This evidence attests to the fact that all cultures are one race, descended from Noah and ultimately Adam.

A few years later, this same missionary recounted the situation when an old Aboriginal elder told him that the Aborigines had a story handed down for generations, that woman was made while man was asleep. Remembering our conversation, the missionary opened the Bible and read the account of the creation of Eve.

The Aboriginal said, "How come you have the same story we have — but your story is better." The missionary was able to lead this man to the Lord Jesus Christ.

CREATION
EVANGELISM

Q. *When did the apostle Paul use creation evangelism to emphasize the message of the Cross?*

A. In Acts 17, we read the account of Paul's ministry to the Greeks. He went to Mars Hill to preach to the Greek philosophers.

When Paul preached the message of the Cross and Resurrection, the Greek philosophers responded by rejecting this teaching as foolish.

However, as we read the rest of this chapter, we find that Paul used a method of evangelism that caused some of these people not only to listen to what Paul said — but they were actually converted!

You see, the Greek culture was permeated with evolutionary ideas, many centuries before Darwin. They had no concept of the Creator God that Paul was presenting to them. They had no basis in their culture to understand that they were sinners, under the curse of Genesis 3.

To reach this evolution-based culture, Paul carefully explained the message of creation. He opposed their wrong ideas. He then presented the message of the Cross again.

Christians need to wake up and understand that our western culture has become like the Greeks. Whole generations have been indoctrinated in evolution — they don't understand sin. Until someone restores the foundation of creation and the fall of man, they'll not understand the gospel.

Q. *Was the apostle Paul successful as an evangelist?*

A. In Acts 17, Paul preached the message of the Cross to the Greeks in Athens. At first, they all mocked him. You see, they had no understanding in their culture of the Creator God . . . or of sin. They also believed in evolutionary ideas. Paul had to teach them about the true history of the world and the origin of sin before they understood the gospel.

As a result of Paul explaining the gospel from the beginning, some were converted. Because only a few of these Greeks trusted the Lord, some people think that Paul was not very successful. After all, in Acts 2 Peter saw thousands come to the Lord after he preached.

However, Paul was VERY successful. He was dealing with a culture that had no foundation for the Christian message. He was teaching outright pagans. Peter, on the other hand, was teaching people who already believed in the true God.

This should be a lesson for us. Because our own culture today is more like the Greeks, don't expect massive conversions as in generations past.

Q. *How can evangelism be harder than 2,000 years ago when Paul preached Christ to the Gentiles?*

A. It's true that Paul had a hard job preaching the gospel to people who didn't have the foundations of the gospel that the Jews had. For instance, the Jews believed in the Creator God and understood about sin and the need for repentance. Their stumbling block was accepting Jesus Christ as the Messiah.

However, the people Paul preached to, by and large, had no concept of a Creator God or the meaning of sin. This is why the Greeks at Athens first thought the message of the Cross was foolishness.

In our cultures today, we have generations coming through education systems that are devoid of the knowledge of God. These people are like Greeks, with no foundation to understand the gospel. However, there is a difference — the education system today largely teaches AGAINST Christianity.

We now have a much harder job than Paul, in the sense that we have to counter all the anti-Christian propaganda as well as the intense evolutionary teaching before many will even listen to the claims of the Bible.

Q. *Why was the apostle Peter so successful as an evangelist?*

A. I want you to think about this question. If we preached the same message Peter did to our western culture today — would we get the same response?

Let's be honest. Evangelistic crusades don't get the same results today as they did years ago. In fact, statistics bear out that most of those who go forward at such meetings today already have a church background. We only see a few REAL first-time commitments.

Why don't we see thousands being saved at a meeting as in Peter's day?

Well, when Peter was preaching to the Jews, or to people already familiar with the Jewish beliefs — he was preaching to a creation-based culture. These people understood about the Creator God. They had God's law — so they knew what sin was.

Today, however, we have generations that've been taught evolution as fact. They don't understand there's an absolute authority. By and large, they have no concept of sin. They really need the answers in Genesis before they can understand and respond to the gospel.

Q. *What's wrong with teaching Bible stories?*

A. I praise the Lord that my Dad and Mom taught me all the stories from the Bible. But here's the problem.

We live in a world today where the Bible is openly attacked. Evolutionary scientists claim that science has disproved the Bible's historicity. Now the trouble is that most Sunday school material, for instance, JUST teaches kids Bible stories.

What I mean is this: at church, children and adults are taught about the feeding of the five thousand, Paul's missionary journeys, Jonah and the whale, and so on. However, when these people go out into the world, the Bible is attacked by such claims as these: science has proved evolution is true, Noah couldn't fit the animals on the ark, ape-men disprove the Bible, science has proven the earth is billions of years old, dinosaurs prove the Bible wrong.

To equip Christians today, we can't JUST teach Bible stories — we need to teach people how to defend the Bible against these secular attacks, so people will be challenged to listen to and believe these Bible stories.

Q. *Is there a communication problem today that makes a gospel presentation more difficult?*

A. Yes. Let me give you an example. If someone is going to present the gospel in France, for example, then one needs to communicate in the language people would understand — French. Now that seems obvious.

However, if we're going to present the gospel in an English-speaking country like America, then it seems logical to do so in the English language. Now in a real sense, this is true — BUT — in another sense, many people in America don't speak the same language. Confusing?

But let me explain. Generations ago, most people in America went to church. They understood Christian jargon. They knew what was meant by sin and trusting in the Lord Jesus Christ.

However, in today's world, increasing numbers of people have grown up outside the church and have been heavily indoctrinated against the Bible by evolutionary humanists. These people don't understand words like "sin" — nor do they know who Jesus is. The Christian message is like a different language to them.

To teach them the gospel, one would need to start right at the beginning — starting with Genesis.

Q: *When Paul preached to the Greeks, why didn't they understand the gospel message at first?*

A. We read in 1 Corinthians 1:23: *But we preach Christ crucified, unto the Jews a stumbling block, and unto the Greeks foolishness.*

It's fascinating to notice the difference between the way the Jews responded to the gospel in Acts 2 compared to the Greeks in Athens in Acts 17. You see, the Jews understood the meaning of sin and why they sacrificed animals. They also had the law of Moses and thus knew that murder, adultery, and so on were sin.

However, the Greeks were basically evolutionists. They had no concept of the Creator God of the Scriptures and no understanding of sin. So when Paul preached the message of the Cross, they thought it was foolishness.

Paul had to start at the very beginning, from Genesis, to lay the foundation of the gospel before the Greeks understood. He also had to show them that their evolutionary ideas were wrong and to explain about the Creator God.

I believe many people in our culture today are like the Greeks. They don't understand the gospel because they have no concept of the Creator God or sin.

Q. *Is original sin foundational to the gospel?*

A. Well it should be obvious – and yet I find most people in our churches today don't really seem to understand this.

Because people have been brainwashed by evolutionary teaching, many Christians insist that Genesis is not important to the gospel. I've even had many pastors tell me that the most important thing is that people trust in Jesus and it doesn't matter whether they believe in Genesis or not.

I challenged some pastors recently by asking this question: "If someone says they trust in Jesus — whatever that means — but they've not understood that they're a sinner — there's been no repentance — no understanding of a broken relationship with their Creator — then are they truly born again?"

These pastors just looked at me. Finally, some of them said, "Well, no — they must repent of their sin."

Personally, I think our churches are full of people who claim to have "trusted in Jesus" — but they've never understood about sin nor come to repentance before their Creator. I think they've just added Jesus in with all their other gods.

Churches need to be teaching the gospel starting with Genesis.

Q. *What are the 7 Cs and how do we teach them?*

A. The 7 Cs represent the true history of the universe from beginning to end. Let me list them: Creation, Corruption (which is the entrance of sin), Catastrophe (or the flood of Noah's day), Confusion (at the Tower of Babel), Christ, Cross (and the Resurrection), and the Consummation (meaning the new heavens and earth) to come.

When you think about it — everything you teach in Christianity can be placed somewhere on this timeline of history. You see, Christianity is based in history. In fact, I call the Bible the history book of the universe. The Bible is not just a book about religion — it's history!

Sadly, because of the influence of evolutionary teaching, many Christians haven't understood that the Bible is history. Thus, their children grow up not understanding the true history of the world. This is why they don't know what to do with dinosaurs and fossils and so on.

Once Christians accept and understand these 7 Cs, they develop a true Christian way of thinking so they can understand the world. Let's teach our children the true history of the universe beginning with Genesis.

Q. *Why should Christians teach Genesis, especially the first 11 chapters?*

A. The first thing Christians need to realize is that ALL of the New Testament is founded in the Old Testament — and ultimately, ALL of the Old and New Testaments are founded in the first 11 chapters of Genesis.

I've had many Christians tell me that the most important teaching to believe is the message of Christ's death and resurrection. After all, this is central to the gospel. But as I point out to them, the reason for Christ's death and resurrection is actually found in the historical account of the Fall as found in Genesis 3.

Ultimately, directly or indirectly, every single biblical doctrine of theology is founded in the first 11 chapters of Genesis. Think about it. Here are just a few: sin, death, clothing, why Jesus is called the last Adam, marriage, and so on.

Many Christians today try to preach the gospel without Genesis 1–11, and they wonder why people don't understand what it's all about. The Church needs to not only teach the power and hope of the gospel, but the foundation of the gospel right from Genesis 1–11.

Q. *What is chronological teaching?*

A. If we buy a book or a video, think about where we would start. Towards the end? Of course not. We start at the beginning so we'll understand the rest of it.

Now think about Christians. Where do most of them start when they read the Bible? Most begin towards the end, in the New Testament.

This is why I believe so many Christians don't really understand — and thus do not know how to defend — the Christian message.

One of the things we seem to have departed from in the Church is teaching the Bible as a history book. You see, God has revealed to us the history of the universe from the beginning in His written Word. As we read through the Bible, we learn about the major events of history that are important to our understanding of what life and the gospel are all about.

Sadly, I believe that evolutionary indoctrination has stopped many people from reading the Bible chronologically. Thus, we have many in our church who don't really understand Christianity, because they don't have all the Old Testament teaching that explains the gospel fully. Christians need to read the Bible starting at the beginning — Genesis.

Q. *What has plowed ground got to do with the creation-gospel message?*

A. In Matthew 13, we read the parable about the sower and the seed. The seed represents the gospel. The sower wanted to see the seed grow so there could be a harvest. While some of the seed fell in the plowed ground, some fell on other ground. Only the seed that fell on plowed ground grew properly.

I believe that generations ago, our culture had a lot of plowed ground. The homes, churches, and schools taught about the Bible and Christianity. This enabled evangelists to sow the seed and reap a harvest of souls.

However, because of the teaching of evolution, most of this plowed ground has now disappeared. Sadly, when preachers today throw out the seed, by and large, it's falling on rocky and thorny ground. There's very little prepared ground to be receptive to the seed.

If we want to preach the gospel today, we first of all have to plow the ground — we need to remove the trees and rocks of evolution so the ground can be receptive to the gospel.

Q. *Do people ask the same questions about the Bible no matter what the country?*

A. Yes. Over the past 20 years, I've spoken in Japan, Hong Kong, Germany, Belgium, France, Luxembourg, Australia, New Zealand, Canada, all over America, and other places.

The interesting thing to me is that everywhere I speak, no matter what the language, people ask the same questions such as:

> Where did Cain get his wife?
>
> How did Noah fit the animals like dinosaurs on the ark?
>
> Have scientists proved the earth is billions of years old?
>
> How do dinosaurs fit with the Bible?

What this shows to me is that the same arguments have been used against the Bible all around the world. The secular scientists have indoctrinated people to believe that Christians can't answer such questions and therefore the Bible can't be true.

However, these questions CAN be answered. And I've found, that as I've been able to give answers, many people have been challenged to believe the Bible — and many have committed their lives to the Lord. Christians need to be equipped with these answers to effectively witness for the Lord in today's world.

Q. *How can Genesis be a powerful tool to reach pagan cultures with the gospel?*

A. Well, let me give you the example of a missionary organization called New Tribes. They're actually using what we've termed "creation evangelism" in reaching pagan peoples.

New Tribes found that when they just preached the message of Christ on the cross, and His dying for our sins, many tribes didn't understand the message. Instead, New Tribes started with the Book of Genesis, explaining where people came from, what happened in the Garden of Eden, and, therefore, why Jesus came to die on the cross for their sins. Once all of this was explained, these pagan tribes could more fully understand the gospel, and many committed their lives to Christ.

You know what I've discovered? There's not that much difference between approaching those kinds of cultures and our own society today with the gospel. We now have whole generations of young people who've been trained in an education system to think — and believe — apart from God and His Word. They don't understand the message of the Cross until you go to Genesis and explain the origin of all things. With this foundation laid, many more people will understand the wonderful message of Christ's death and resurrection.

Q. *When sharing our faith, where should we begin?*

A. Currently, most Bible colleges and seminaries instruct future missionaries to preach the message of Jesus from the New Testament when they evangelize pagan tribes.

However, missionaries are realizing there is an enormous problem with this limited approach. New Tribes missionaries, for example, thought that they had lots of converts when they preached the message of the Cross and challenged natives to trust in Jesus. They thought that many responded positively. As time went on, though, they realized that, in fact, there were very few real converts at all.

As they investigated this, the New Tribes missionaries realized that because these native people had not heard the account of origins from Genesis, they did not fully understand what it meant that they were sinners. They had no foundation to understand the gospel.

The missionaries then started teaching from the beginning – giving them the details of history from Adam right through to Christ. After doing this, they found many natives made sincere commitments to the Lord — because they now understood the gospel!

We need to follow the same example in our own culture. Increasingly, people don't understand the gospel because they no longer believe the true account of origins and sin in Genesis.

Q: *Is evolution one of the biggest stumbling blocks people have to listening to the gospel?*

A. There's no doubt in my mind from 20 years of ministry around the world, that the teaching of evolution is one of the biggest — if not THE biggest — stumbling block to people being receptive to the gospel of Jesus Christ.

I remember when I was a teacher in Australia's public schools, some of my students questioned me, "Sir, how can you believe the Bible, when it states God made Adam and Eve. Evolution has shown this story to be false."

Once I clearly showed the students that it was evolution that was false, they listened to the claims of the Bible. Some of these young people then committed their lives to the Lord.

We receive testimonies almost daily at our office from people who say that it was evolution that stopped them from becoming a Christian. Just recently I met a colonel in the U.S. military who told me that he became a Christian after reading some of our books that answered his questions about evolution.

Christians would be more effective in their evangelism if they removed this stumbling block of evolution before presenting the gospel.

Q. What does the persecution of Christians in Japan have to do with the creation-evolution issue?

A. While speaking in Japan, I was told by my translator that the Japanese culture has no Christian basis. Because of the prevalence of the Shinto religion, and a belief in many gods — he explained that when I used the word "God," he would have to define who God is — the Creator God, who made and upholds all things.

The translator also told me that most Japanese people would have no concept of what I meant by sin. After all, if they've never heard the account of creation and the Fall in Genesis — how would they understand?

I started to realize that to present the gospel in such a culture — one couldn't just go and preach about sin, Jesus, and the Cross — I'd have to lay down the foundation from Genesis first, so then they would understand the gospel.

You know what hit me? We have generations coming through our education system that are like the Japanese — devoid of the knowledge of God. They, too, need this same approach if we're to proclaim the gospel to them.

Q. *Why is it so difficult to try to reach the Japanese people with the gospel?*

A. I remember the first time I went to Japan to speak. The Japanese translator explained that up until the last world war, Christians were persecuted and killed in Japan. He told me that there was no Christian basis whatsoever in the culture.

He said that when I used the word "God," because of the Shinto religion, the Japanese would understand this as just another god to add to all their others. The translator would need to define God as the CREATOR God.

Also, because evolution is taught as fact through Japan's education system, I would have to show them this was wrong.

He also told me that the Japanese people would not understand sin or who Jesus Christ is so I would have to lay the basics of Christianity from the beginning — starting with Genesis, so they would understand the gospel.

I believe people in our once-Christianized nations are more like the Japanese culture today — the teaching of evolution has removed the foundation of the gospel from their thinking.

Q. *Why are the results of creation evangelism usually not immediate?*

A. Simply put, people can't understand the message of the Cross and Resurrection, if they don't already have an understanding of sin and why Jesus died.

Today, increasing numbers of people have been trained in an education system devoid of the knowledge of God. Evolutionary indoctrination has resulted in many people not having any concept of the loving Creator God of the Bible and the nature of sin.

Creation evangelism is the name given to a powerful method to reach these people. We first need to remove the stumbling block of evolution by showing its fallacies, and then present the truth of the history of the world, beginning with Genesis. Many people have committed their lives to Christ as a result of using this method.

But the results are slow at first. This is because a person has to change his or her whole way of thinking from the foundation up. If we're going to be successful in evangelism in today's secular culture, we need to understand that although results will be slow at first — creation evangelism works!

Q. *Do we need a different style of evangelism because of our new millennium?*

A. Actually, as we start another millennium, it's a good time for people to think about the culture they live in and how successful they really are in reaching people with the gospel.

Personally, I believe our evangelistic methods have needed changing for some time. You see, our once very Christianized nations have become increasingly secular and anti-Christian. As a result, we now have generations who have very little or no Christian foundation. They've been thoroughly indoctrinated in evolution and human-ism . . . and the Bible has been taught against. Thus, these people don't understand about sin and the message of Jesus Christ. They think the Bible is an outdated religious book disproved by science.

The trouble is, most Christians still approach the culture as if people understand Christian jargon and accept the basics of Christianity from the Bible.

In presenting the gospel today, we need to remove the stumbling block of evolution and teach people about the true origin of man and the entrance of sin. Then they WILL understand the gospel. In other words, we have to start right back at the beginning.

Q. *In what way has our culture changed, and why is this change important to understand?*

A. When I attended public school in Australia, I remember our principal having prayer with us at the start of each day. I also recall my teachers reading Bible stories to us before we started our classwork. I think everyone heard about the Ten Commandments.

However, things are very different today. I don't know of any public schools that have prayer or Bible readings as part of their daily schedule. Sadly today, students, by and large, are taught that there is no God, and that we're all evolved animals.

The same is true of countries like America and England — in fact, probably all western nations.

You see, years ago, when evangelists preached the message of the Cross, people in our culture understood the message. They knew about God's law — about sin. They understood who Jesus was.

However, things are very different today. Our culture has changed from one based on God's Word to one based on evolution. Many Christians don't understand that unless we see the foundation change back again, we will not be able to communicate the gospel message effectively.

Q: *How is creation evangelism a powerful tool for preaching the gospel?*

A. I believe that creation evangelism is one of the most powerful tools today to reach the lost with the gospel of Jesus Christ. And yet, most Christians don't even know about this biblically based method to evangelize.

I speak to thousands of people each year around the globe. I often ask the following question of audiences: "How many of you have tried to preach the gospel to someone — but they reject what you say by bringing up something to do with evolution?"

Without exception, I find a large number of hands go up. I then point out to these people that the teaching of evolution is one of the biggest barriers to people being responsive to the gospel. For them, science has supposedly proved the Bible wrong. So why should they listen when you talk about the message of the Cross?

We've found time and time again that when you refute their evolutionary arguments, and show them that the Bible's account of creation can logically be defended — they'll often listen to the gospel. As a result, we've seen many come to Christ our Creator!

Q. *Is the creation-evolution controversy important in sharing our faith with non-Christians?*

A. Christians do need to understand that evolution is one of the biggest stumbling blocks today in presenting the gospel message.

I travel to the United Kingdom every year and often have an opportunity to speak to Christian university students who have been sharing their faith on campus. In Edinburgh, Scotland, a number of Christian students approached me after I'd given a lecture. They said, "We realized something tonight. When we've been trying to witness to our non-Christian friends at the university, they always seem to bring up the same two questions." I stopped them and offered a guess: "Would those questions be: 'creation and evolution' and also 'death and suffering?' "

"Yes," they responded with surprise. "Those two questions come up over and over again. But we've been told by our churches to just ignore them and just let our friends know that Jesus died for their sins on the cross."

These students realized that they must have answers to these questions. You see, evolution is often a stumbling block for the non-believer. The world needs to know that evolution is not a fact. Then they'll be more open to the gospel message.

How can we witness effectively? The answer's in Genesis: start with God as Creator.

Q. *What was the stumbling block the Jews had to the gospel?*

A. Before I explain, let's read 1 Corinthians 1:23: *But we preach Christ crucified, unto the Jews a stumbling block, and unto the Greeks foolishness.*

Paul is explaining here that the message of Christ and the cross was a stumbling block to the Jews. You see, the Jews rejected Jesus Christ as the Messiah. However, the Jews at that time did believe in God the Creator. They also had the law of Moses and understood the meaning of sin. In other words, they had the foundation of the gospel.

Now on the Day of Pentecost in Acts 2, when Peter preached to the Jews, his main message concerned the fact that they crucified the Son of God. He taught them that Jesus was the Messiah. Thousands were converted.

Years ago, our own culture was like the Jews – people understood about the Creator and sin — so they could understand the gospel as the Jews did. But our culture does not have this foundation any more — it's not like the Jews now. Before we can preach about the Cross, people need to be taught the foundations of the gospel from Genesis.

Q. *How is today's society like the Greeks?*

A. There's no doubt that America was once a great Christian nation. In fact, years ago, the Bible was taught in its public schools. Prayer and the teaching of the Ten Commandments were a part of the daily school program. Most people respected the Bible and understood the meaning of sin and knew about Jesus Christ.

In other words, like the Jews, the foundation of the gospel was inherent in American culture. That's why evangelists could preach about sin and repentance and see thousands come to Christ.

However, things are very different today in America and many other once-Christian nations. By and large, the Bible and prayer are not allowed in government schools. Evolution is taught as fact. Today when evangelists preach the message of sin and repentance, there's an increasing number of people who don't understand what they're talking about. They're like the Greek culture that had no foundation for the gospel.

To reach these people with the gospel, we need to follow Paul's example in Acts 17. We should oppose their evolutionary ideas and explain about the true God and the origin of sin — by starting with Genesis.

Evolution

vs.

Creation

Q. What is theistic evolution and how does death rule out this view?

A. Many Christians have been thoroughly indoctrinated in the ideas of evolution and millions of years of history. As a result, they believe that God must have used the evolutionary process as part of His creative acts in producing living things.

Now there are many fatal flaws with this view. One of the most obvious concerns the issue of death. Evolution involves a process of death and struggle over millions of years. As animals kill and eat each other, and many groups die out — eventually the animals (as we know them) and man evolved. The record of the death of billions of creatures in the fossil record is supposed to be the record of the history of life, according to evolution.

However, the answers in Genesis make it plain that the world was perfect before Adam's sin – there was no death, disease, bloodshed, or suffering. The animals originally were vegetarian. Death and bloodshed came into the world AFTER sin. This fact is foundational to the gospel and the reason Jesus died on the cross. The origin of death definitely rules out the compromise view of theistic evolution.

Q. *What is "progressive creation" and how does death disallow this view?*

A. Through our media and public education system, people have been bombarded with the idea that the earth is millions of years in age. As a result, many Christians have tried to fit the millions of years with the creation account in Genesis. One such position is called "progressive creation." This is the belief that God created billions of creatures over millions of years, but kept replacing them as they died out.

This view accepts the idea that the fossil layers are the records of the history of life over millions of years.

However, progressive creation is a compromise position that actually destroys the foundation of the gospel. It's a view that teaches that death, disease, violence, bloodshed, and suffering over millions of years are part of the way God creates. This makes God out to be a cruel ogre — not the loving God described in the Bible.

Also, our answers in Genesis teach us that death came AFTER Adam's sin. You cannot reconcile the Genesis account of the origin of death and the supposed millions of years of history. To do so is to undermine the very gospel and the reason why Jesus died for us.

Q. *What is the "gap theory"?*

A. Back in the early 1800s, certain people started to popularize the idea that the fossil record was formed slowly, over millions of years. A very prominent theologian decided that he would fit these supposed millions of years in a gap between the first two verses of Genesis. This became known as the "gap theory."

The classic gap theory has a world of people living before this present one, ruled by Lucifer, who then rebelled. God judged them with a flood called Lucifer's flood, supposedly forming the fossil layers. Then God recreated everything in six days.

People who accept this believe that the earth really is billions of years old. But this is not true. The majority of dating methods, in fact, give dates far YOUNGER than evolutionists require!

Secondly, if the fossils were formed BEFORE Adam sinned — then there was death, disease, and suffering BEFORE Adam rebelled. This doesn't fit with Scripture.

Also, if EVERYTHING God created (which included the angels) was VERY GOOD at the end of the sixth day of creation — how could there be rebellion in the universe before that time?

No, let's give up the gap theory.

Q. *Can we believe in both evolution and the Bible?*

A. Unfortunately, my experiences have shown me that probably a majority of Christians — and the majority of pastors — accept some form of evolution and add it to the Bible. For example, they say that God could've used evolutionary processes over millions of years to bring about plants, animals, and finally man.

But this view — called "theistic evolution" — is actually destructive to the very gospel message itself. Of course, I'm not saying that people who believe in "theistic evolution" are not Christians. Actually, they're very inconsistent, and probably haven't thought through the logical implications of their position.

The Bible clearly teaches that when God created Adam and Eve, the world was perfect. There was no death and bloodshed. But because of the sin of Adam, God brought death as a judgment into the world. Of course, He provided a means by which man could be reconciled to his Creator. But if you believe in evolution, you believe that God used death and bloodshed over millions of years as a way to bring man into existence. This actually destroys the foundation of the gospel message.

The answer's in Genesis — there's no room for evolution in the Bible.

Q: *Why can't Christians believe that the days of creation were not six 24-hour days?*

A. Actually, this is a very important question, and reveals our attitude toward Scripture. Sadly, the majority of Christians — and a majority of pastors — don't accept that the days of creation were six, literal 24-hour days. But I've found that their major reason has nothing to do with what the Bible teaches, but everything to do with the opinions of man.

Now what do I mean?

Constantly people tell me that the days of creation can't be six literal days because scientists have proved that the earth is billions of years old. Actually, they haven't shown that at all. You see, dating methods have all sorts of assumptions built into their equations by scientists who are fallible men who weren't there at the beginning.

So, here's a challenging question: Why are Christians so quick to accept the words of men who don't know everything, who weren't there at the beginning, and use their fallen brains to judge God's Word, instead of accepting the fact that God knows everything and He has always been there?

If we take God at his word, the answer is in Genesis: God created in only six 24-hour days!

Q. *Why are some theologians proudly announcing that they no longer believe in the bodily resurrection of Christ?*

A. You may remember that *Time* magazine did a story on theologians associated with what's called the "Jesus Seminar." They gathered together and voted on certain theological issues. Using colored marbles, they even voted on the resurrection of Christ. They had enough of the right colored marbles to declare that Jesus did not rise from the dead!

Why is this happening, particularly in America where the Resurrection was once accepted by the population?

I'll guarantee that you'll find one thing in common with these theologians. They will not believe in a literal Genesis, and they'll have compromised with evolution in some way. You see, if you believe in six, 24-hour days of creation, a global flood, and a literal first Adam, you'll have no trouble believing in a literal last Adam — that's Jesus Christ, whose bodily resurrection is central to the gospel message. However, if evolution is true, and thus the first Adam is just a myth, then ultimately the last Adam, Christ, will be also.

Why do these theologians reject the Resurrection? The answer actually goes hand in hand with their rejection of the Book of Genesis!

Q. *How does Satan convince people not to trust the Bible?*

A. Let's turn to 2 Corinthians 11:3. This is the passage that outlines a warning for us concerning the methods Satan will use to get people to disbelieve the Bible. Here, Paul warns that Satan will use the same method as he did on Eve not to believe what God has said.

In Genesis, Satan created doubt by asking the question: "Did God really say that?" Thousands of years later, the same question is being asked by Christians when they read Genesis. For example, they wonder "Did God really say that it was a six-day creation? Did God really say there was a worldwide flood?" and so on.

This doubt is often created because of the teaching of evolution. And Satan knows that if you can get people to doubt Genesis, which is the foundational book of the Bible, then it can lead to questioning the rest of Scripture. That's why we need to believe the answers from Genesis, and not let Satan — or the evolutionists — cause us to doubt God's Word.

Q. *Is it possible that words in the Hebrew language have changed meanings, making Genesis unreliable?*

A. A man once called me to say that we shouldn't insist that God created everything in six 24-hour days because the Hebrew word for "day" in Genesis may have changed its meaning. Therefore, he argued that it may not have been a literal day when the Hebrew word for "day" was first used.

I explained to this person that if this was so — and using his logic — it would be possible that every word in the Bible in the original languages may have changed meaning. Therefore, you wouldn't be able to trust anything the Bible said.

It needs to be known that our English language is really a mixture of a number of languages and does tend to be rather "plastic." However, Hebrew is a very stable language. I'm sure that over the years, as the scribes painstakingly copied the Scriptures, that they would've made a special note if a word had drastically changed its meaning.

The Hebrew word for "day" in the context of Genesis means an ordinary day. It's so sad that many Christians will try anything not to believe what the Bible makes so clear. They should take their answers from Genesis, not fallible men.

Q. Should Christians believe in a "big bang"?

A. First of all, we must look at what God says to us about what occurred in the past. After all, He's the only eyewitness to the origin of the universe.

When we read the Book of Genesis, we discover that God created the earth covered with water — before He created the sun. You see, in the big bang theory, the earth was formed after the sun, and at first it was a hot, molten blob. Thus, the Bible's account of the origins of the universe and man's story of evolution are in total conflict. This means the big bang is wrong.

A creation scientist named Dr. Russ Humphreys has researched the big bang thoroughly. He's discovered many assumptions that most of us have never heard of. For example, he found that it doesn't assume any center to the universe. He also found that if you do assume there is a center, and that the universe has an edge, and you put all this information into the equations of Einstein, you get a totally different model of the universe — and it fits with what the Bible teaches!

Is the big bang true? The answer's in Genesis. God created the earth before the sun. The big bang is wrong.

Q. *What kind of big bang should Christians believe in?*

A. Well, when people ask me if I believe in the big bang, I answer, "Sure do — are you getting ready for it?"

Now let me explain. I certainly don't believe the big bang brought the universe into existence. You see, this theory has the stars and sun coming into existence before the earth — but the Bible states that the earth was created BEFORE the sun and stars.

However, I do believe the Bible does talk about a big bang. In 2 Peter 3:10 we read:

> But the day of the Lord will come as a thief in the night; in the which the heavens shall pass away with a great noise, and the elements shall melt with fervent heat, the earth also and the works that are therein shall be burned up.

This, of course, is talking about the coming judgment by fire, when there'll be a great noise. This is the real big bang — the final judgment on this earth.

Are you ready for the big bang to come?

Q. *What's a double conversion?*

A. Well, Dr. James Allen, a retired lecturer in genetics from a university in South Africa, recounts how he was spiritually converted — and also converted from believing in evolution to creation.

Dr. Allen was an evolutionist for 40 years and taught evolutionary genetics. He was convinced that evolution explained the similarities that exist in living things, and that all living things share the same system of genetic coding — DNA.

One day his wife asked him, "Is there any reason why God should not have created all forms of life on the basis of a universal code?"

The more he started thinking about what she said — the more God spoke to his heart. Feeling somewhat humbled, he found himself thinking that maybe God did create all forms of life on the basis of a universal genetic code. *After all*, he thought, *why should we expect our Creator God to do otherwise.*

If a professor who taught evolution for 40 years can so easily give it up, it really speaks volumes for the fact that evolution is just a belief. It's not science. The true account of origins comes from our answers in Genesis.

Q. *Should the majority view be important to the creation-evolution debate?*

A. There are many instances where the majority view has been proven to be wrong. Doctors once believed that they didn't need to wash their hands before doing an operation — but the majority were wrong.

At one seminar, a pastor said to me, "But how can you believe in a young earth, when the majority of scientists believe it's billions of years old?"

I replied, "Well, pastor, just because the majority believe it, doesn't mean it's true."

He then said, "I know that — but surely the majority couldn't be that wrong?"

I then stated, "Pastor, the Bible tells us there are more on the broad way than the narrow way."

This man said again, "But surely the majority of scientists couldn't be that wrong?"

I responded, "Remember pastor, the majority of scientists in Noah's day didn't survive the flood!"

The majority opinion should never be used as a basis for determining truth. Really, the only absolute authority we have is the Word of God — beginning with answers in Genesis.

Q. *How could an ant and tree work together?*

A. You know, such cooperation between ants and acacia trees is well known in Africa.

The fierce soldier ants actually guard the tree from being eaten by plant- and tree-eating animals and protect it from other threats. In return, the ants get food and shelter from the tree.

However, a problem arises when the acacia trees need insects to pollinate them. Remember: the ants guard against all intruders. Well, it just so happens that at just the right time, when the acacia flowers need to be pollinated, the tree sends out a chemical signal to keep the ants away!

This allows pollinating insects to arrive at the flowers without being attacked. So, the flowers are pollinated and seeds are produced. Soon after, the ants return to resume their "guard patrol" of the tree.

This is just one of many such examples we see in the animal and plant kingdom. There's no way such relationships could have developed by chance, random processes over millions of years.

As we say at Answers in Genesis — It's designed to do what it does do, and what it does do it does do well — doesn't it — don't you think?

Q. *How does the platypus provide special evidence for creation?*

A. This fascinating little animal, by the way, only lives "down under." Yet, people all over the world are intrigued by it.

The platypus was first discovered in 1797. It was sent to England where British scientists thought it was a fraud stitched together by Chinese taxidermists. You see, the platypus is an animal with a bill like a duck and a beaver-like tail. It has hair like a bear, webbed feet like an otter, claws like a reptile, lays eggs like a turtle, has spurs like a rooster, and poison like a snake. You can see why scientists first thought it was a fraud!

The platypus is a real problem for the evolutionists. They believe animals have evolved into other animals over millions of years, so the question is: Which animal did the platypus evolve from? It would have to be just about everything! I think that every time an evolutionist looks at the platypus, God must smile. Maybe He created it just for them.

So the platypus did not evolve. The answer is in Genesis. The Creator God of the Bible designed all animals, including the platypus.

Q. *How can a crab climb trees?*

A. Actually, the story is even more strange than that. This crab is the robber crab, and it can measure two feet long. It's also a monstrous problem for the evolutionist!

If you visit Christmas Island in the Indian Ocean, you'll find a crab that's two feet long from head to tail. It climbs coconut trees, snips off coconuts, and eats them. It's not really the sort of creature you'd like to meet in the dark, is it?

What worries the evolutionists is not that we have a crab that climbs trees, but that this crab is one of about 39,000 known species of creatures that are called "crustaceans." Here's the interesting thing: evolutionists admit they have never, ever found any in-between — or transitional form — for crustaceans. There's absolutely no evidence for any evolutionary ancestors for creatures like this huge, tree-climbing crab. Evolutionists have no idea how to explain this crab's evolution.

I'm glad I get my answers from the Creator, who told us all we need to know in His Word about how these creatures came to be.

Q: *What does a bat in a stalagmite have to do with the creation-evolution question?*

A. Many people believe that it takes hundreds or thousands of years for stalactites and stalagmites to grow in caves. Thus, they believe that the many limestone caves around the world must be very, very old. But let's look at the Sequoia Caverns in Alabama. Researchers have measured stalactites growing at the rate of one inch per year. In other places, they've been measured to grow up to three inches per year.

In October of 1953, the *National Geographic* magazine published a photograph of a bat that had fallen on a stalagmite in the famous Carlsbad Caverns in New Mexico. The stalagmite had grown so fast, it was able to preserve the bat before it decomposed. Obviously, this didn't take millions of years!

There are many such evidences from around our world that contradict the idea of millions of years of earth history. But our answers from Genesis provide us with information to explain limestone caves and their stalagmites. Noah's flood would have deposited layers of limestone all around the world. As the waters from the flood ran off, they would have formed cave systems, and then stalagmites and stalactites.

The evidence fits with Genesis, not evolution!

Q. *What's the significance of galaxies winding up too fast?*

A. Actually, the fact that galaxies do wind themselves up is a BIG problem for those who believe the universe is billions of years old.

You see, the stars of our own galaxy, the Milky Way, rotate around its center with different speeds. The stars on the inside rotate faster that the outer ones. Now our galaxy is a spiral shape. So, because of the difference in the rotation of the stars, over time, the spiral will wind itself up until there's no spiral left at all!

Evolutionists claim that our galaxy is at least 10 billion years old. Now here's the dilemma for evolutionists. On the basis of the speed at which the spirals of the galaxy are winding-up — it could only be a few hundred million years old at the most.

And of course, if God created the galaxy with a spiral shape to start with, then it could only be thousands of years old.

This winding up problem applies to MANY galaxies in our universe. The only solution is to believe the answers in Genesis — that God created a fully functioning universe just a few thousand years ago.

Q. What's the problem with comets disintegrating too quickly?

A. Actually, there's no problem with comets disintegrating quickly — except that this fact flies in the face of the evolutionists who believe our solar system is at least 5 billion years old.

Let me explain. According to evolutionary theory, comets are supposed to be the same age as the solar system — about 5 billion years. Now each time a comet orbits close to the sun, it loses much of its material. There is NO WAY it could survive much longer than about 100,000 years. On this same basis, many comets have to be younger than even 10,000 years. The point is, the disintegration of comets indicates the universe is very YOUNG. Is there a solution?

One way evolutionists try to get around this is to propose a special cloud beyond Pluto that somehow gives birth to comets. No one has seen this cloud — but evolutionists believe it must be there because they insist the solar system IS billions of years old.

Really, comets fit in nicely with a universe just a few thousand years old — as our answers in Genesis teach us.

Q. *How does the exploration of the universe prove evolutionists have limited knowledge?*

A. You know, sometimes I wonder how people can keep clinging to evolution, when scientists keep finding evidence that contradicts it.

Evolutionists claim the solar system is about 5 billion years old. However, when the rings of a planet like Uranus were investigated, scientists realized that these rings couldn't last any longer than around 1 billion years.

Because of this, they had to come up with theories to try to explain how the rings could be continually repaired. One scientist suggested that the rings might grind against each other in some way that continually creates new particles.

He said that if there was no process to regenerate the rings, then any dust or rings that existed billions of years ago, would long since have been removed by the atmospheric drag. In other words, because they BELIEVE the solar system is billions of years old — they BELIEVE there MUST be some explanation to renew the rings.

But there's another and better explanation — the solar system isn't that old. Over and over we find the evidence fits with a young age for our universe — just thousands of years.

Q. *How did the planet Venus surprise scientists?*

A. Evolutionists believe the solar system is at least 4.5 billion years old. Therefore, as they send spacecraft into outer space, they fully expect to find evidence that the solar system is billions of years old.

Now the Magellan spacecraft sent back some wonderful data about the surface of Venus. One of the scientists involved described this material as "spectacular," and that it continues "to amaze everyone."

But do you know what was the most amazing thing of all? The information they received showed little evidence that the craters of Venus had degraded, that the terrain was highly eroded, or that there was local volcanism.

So what does this mean? Well, the landscape looks young — it doesn't appear to have been there for billions of years.

What's the answer then? As we say so often — the answer's in Genesis! The planets were made on the fourth day of creation — around six thousand years ago.

You know what I predict? I predict that the more data scientists get from spacecraft — the more they will be surprised — and that's because evolution is NOT true.

Q. *Do the earth's continents erode too fast for the evolutionists?*

A. Yes! There are numerous processes that reveal that there is no way the earth could be billions of years old.

Did you know that scientists have been able to calculate that each year, water and winds erode about 25 billion tons of dirt and rock from the continents? This material eventually ends up in the ocean.

Now at this rate, geologists can calculate that it would only take around 15 million years to erode all the land above sea level. But this is a major dilemma for the evolutionists. You see, most of the land is supposed to have been above the sea level for HUNDREDS OF MILLIONS OF YEARS.

So, how do evolutionists get around this? They have to propose all sorts of complex theories concerning new land being pushed up over millions of years to replace the eroded material. Why don't they believe the obvious!

What makes most sense is to just believe the answers in Genesis — the land is not that old. In fact, the very first dry land was made on day three of the creation week about 6,000 years ago.

Q: *Who has a problem with the shortage of sediment on the sea floors?*

A. Actually, it's a problem for people who believe the oceans are hundreds of millions of years old.

The latest evolutionary theories in geology say our ocean floors are at least 200 million years old. The oceans supposedly formed slowly, they say, as the earth cooled down after the supposed big bang.

However, at the present rate at which sediment is transported into the ocean from the land, it should be miles thick on the ocean floor. But scientists have discovered that the average thickness is only about 800 feet. Now if you assume no sediment to start with, then this thickness would've formed in less than 15 million years — much less than the evolutionist-needed 200 million years.

But biblical creationists don't believe that the oceans are 15 millions years old. So how do they explain even this 800 feet of sediment?

Well, consider that Noah's flood would've added most of this sediment anyway. In other words, the thickness of the sediment on the ocean floor can be explained within a few thousand years — just as we'd expect, based on our answers in Genesis.

Q. *How is the salt content of the ocean another problem for evolutionists who believe in billions of years?*

A. You could say that the oceans are far too salty for the evolutionists' taste! The amount of salt in the oceans rules out their supposed billions of years' age.

Scientists have been able to calculate that each year rivers and other sources dump over 450 million tons of sodium, mainly in the form of salt, into the ocean. They've also calculated that only 27 percent of this sodium manages to get back out of the sea each year.

Now if we make the assumption that the oceans had NO sodium to start with — then the amount in the oceans today would have accumulated in less than 42 million years. If we are VERY generous with the figures, we can allow up to 62 million years. However, evolutionists believe the oceans are 3 BILLION years old.

Evolutionists have no real explanation for this. On the other hand, creationists believe that God would have created the oceans with some salt, and Noah's flood probably added much more. The answers in Genesis can easily account for the salt in just thousands of years.

Q. *What does the rapid decay of the earth's magnetic field have to do with the creation-evolution issue?*

A. Many of us are aware that the earth's magnetic field is a good navigational aid and a shield from space particles — but it's also very powerful evidence against the evolutionists' belief in billions of years for the age of the earth.

Scientists have discovered that the earth's magnetic field has steadily decreased by a factor of 2.7 over the past 1,000 years. In fact, measurements since 1835 have shown that the field is decaying at 5 percent per century.

Now if you take the present rate at which the magnetic field is decaying, and extrapolate this backwards, a big problem arises for evolutionists. You see, the current that produces the magnetic field could not have been decaying for more than 10,000 years, or else its original strength would've been large enough to melt the earth! This means the earth must be younger than 10,000 years.

Of course our answers in Genesis tell us that the earth can be no older than around 6,000 years.

The more scientists research our planet — the more they find the evidence fits with what the Bible says — NOT evolution.

Q. *Where is all the helium in our atmosphere?*

A. This is a BIG problem if you believe the earth is billions of years old!

Most people have heard of radioactive materials — like uranium. Now all naturally occurring families of radioactive elements generate helium as they decay. As a result, if this decay has been going on for billions of years as evolutionists claim, there should be an enormous amount of helium in the atmosphere.

However, even if scientists take into account the amount of helium that slowly escapes from the atmosphere — and if the assumption is made that there was no helium in the atmosphere to start with — then it would actually take LESS THAN two million years to accumulate the small amount of helium that we find present today.

This is MUCH younger than the five BILLION years evolutionists claim for the age of the earth.

If we assume there was some helium present from the time of creation, then the amount of helium today fits with our answers in Genesis — the earth is just thousands of years old. You cannot believe in billions of years!

Q. *Does millions of years of erosion form a river valley?*

A. It can seem that way because we're looking at processes that go on in the river valley today. Right now those rivers seem relatively peaceful at the bottom of the valley. But things in the past have been very different.

For example, I once stood on the rim of the Grand Canyon with an evolutionist who said, "Look at this canyon. A long time and a little bit of water carved out this canyon."

Well, I stood there and responded, "No, I think it was a lot of water and just a little bit of time that eroded this canyon."

You see, I believe there truly was a worldwide flood in our past, perhaps just four to five thousand years ago. Evolutionists, however, believe that slow processes over millions of years shaped most of our planet's surface.

Creationists who get their answers from the Book of Genesis have been telling the evolutionists all along that the canyon formed quickly. While many evolutionists are beginning to agree with us regarding the canyon, we need to continue to counter the evolutionary brainwashing in our educational systems and the media.

Q. *Did it take millions of years to form the huge oil deposits around our globe?*

A. Let me give you an example from my homeland of Australia. Between Australia and the island state of Tasmania is a body of water called Bass Strait. Many companies are extracting large quantities of oil and gas from under this body of water. Scientists have also found that the large deposits of coal that are visible on the mainland actually dip down under the Bass Strait.

Well, here's what is fascinating: Scientists have found that both the oil and the gas have formed from the waxes, resins, and saps that are in coal deposits. These researchers took samples of the coal and subjected them to conditions such as those in the rocks beneath the strait. They were actually able to produce good quality oil and gas in just one or two days!

Why is there so much oil today? The answer's in Genesis. The flood of Noah just a few thousand years ago buried billions of tons of plants, and this has become the source of most of our oil deposits.

Q: *Does carbon dating prove the earth is old?*

A. If I'm on a talk show long enough, that question almost always pops up. And the question doesn't come just from skeptics. I remember when a pastor said, "You creationists have to believe that fossils are millions of years old."

I asked, " Why?"

He said, "Because carbon dating proves this."

I would venture to guess that even the average Christian thinks that carbon dating has something to do with dating the earth to be millions of years old. Actually, it has only to do with thousands of years. Though evolutionary dating methods like uranium-lead or potassium-argon come up with dates of millions of years, they really can't be trusted. Some of our own scientists have shown that these dating methods can sometimes get dates ranging from zero years to millions of years . . . in just one rock layer! You see, most people don't understand that before evolutionary scientists even try to use their dating methods, they already believe that the fossils are millions of years old.

We believe that most of the fossils the evolutionists are trying to date were formed during the time of Noah's flood — only thousands of years ago. That answer is found in Genesis.

Q. *Is coal a result of Noah's flood just thousands of years ago rather than of a slow process over millions of years?*

A. I believe that most coal deposits are the result of the flood of Noah's day — not millions of years of slow processes.

The theory that coal formed in swamps over millions of years just doesn't fit with the evidence. Peat swamps that we observe today are totally different in composition and texture than coal deposits. In these swamps we find mainly roots and a texture like mashed potatoes.

However, coal deposits have trees, bark, and other material giving it a totally different texture.

In my homeland of Australia, many of the coal deposits consist largely of pine trees that don't grow in swamps. Some of these trees are enormous — many feet in diameter. And these trees are in coal deposits that are hundreds of feet thick.

The only explanation that fits what we observe in coal deposits is that enormous quantities of plant material, including massive trees, were washed into place. This would require a lot of force and a lot of water. The event of Noah's flood makes sense of this evidence — and gives us the real answers!

Q. *How could oil be a result of Noah's flood?*

A. You know, over and over again, I've found that things we've been led to believe took millions of years have instead been shown to be explained in a very short time scale.

Oil is just another one of those examples. It's true that most people think oil takes millions of years to form. However, in Washington state, researchers have been able to convert sewage into usable oil. So, if this can be done easily in the present world — what's to say it couldn't happen easily in nature?

Well, scientists have now observed oil forming on the ocean bottom in the Gulf of California. Heat from volcanoes has caused rapid breakdown of organic debris to form oil, similar to crude oils.

Scientists in Australia have also been able to form oil and gas from coal in a lab in a relatively short period of time.

All this fits with the idea that plant and other organic material buried during the flood, and heat generated by volcanic action, could easily account for the oil deposits.

Q. *How can hard rock layers be bent and not broken?*

A. This brings up just another of the many evidences consistent with a belief in a young earth.

There are many places where we find layers of rock that are sometimes thousands of feet thick — yet they're bent and folded into shapes that are like hairpins. Now evolutionary geologists would tell us that these layers of rock solidified — or hardened — for hundreds of millions of years BEFORE they were bent.

But there's an insurmountable problem with this. You see, these rock layers haven't cracked. It's as if they were like "play dough," so they could be folded without breaking.

This means these layers had to be bent before they hardened. In other words, this had to happen less than a thousand years after they were deposited.

What's the answer? Well, our answers in Genesis provide the solution. Noah's flood laid down the rock layers just a few thousand years ago. Then sometime after the flood, while the layers were still soft, movements in the earth's crust bent the layers. Eventually the layers hardened.

Those who believe in millions of years have to disregard the obvious — the earth is young!

Q. *Can you give an example of an evolutionary experiment that failed?*

A. This is a real-life experiment that most people are not aware of.

Because of their evolutionary worldview, Hitler and Nietzsche thought they could produce a superior "master race" by selective breeding of the German Aryan bloodline. Because of this belief, a group of blond-haired, blue-eyed Germans immigrated to a remote area of Paraguay to carry out what they called a "purification and rebirth of the human race."

However, after only half a century and three generations later, their experiment lay in ruins. Because of mistakes (called mutations) in our genes resulting from sin and the Curse, the close inbreeding of this small group meant that the mutations were concentrated in these few individuals. As a result, they bred a generation of people who are mentally very slow.

Now had these people started their thinking with the answers in Genesis instead of evolution, they would have looked at the world differently. They would have understood that only the first two people were perfect before sin. They would have realized that sin affected everything, including our genes. They would have also known why God brought in the laws against close inter-marriage at the time of Moses.

Again, evolution fails the test!

Q. *How can the earth be less than 10 thousand years old if the Aborigines of Australia date back 60 thousand years?*

A. The problem is not with Scripture, but in poor evolutionary science.

Evolutionists claim that the Australian Aborigines have been around for at least 60,000 years.

But if we get our answers from Genesis, we realize they couldn't have been in Australia much longer than four to five thousand years — since the time of Noah's flood. After the Tower of Babel, the ancestors of the Aborigines made their way to Australia.

And you know what? The more we look at the evidence, the more we discover that it fits with a biblical time frame, not an evolutionary one.

Recently in Australia, evolutionists found some stone tools used by an aboriginal culture. They were dated to be, supposedly, 13,000 years. On one of the tools, however, they found the protein "hemoglobin," which is what gives blood its red color. But hemoglobin can't last 13,000 years! In fact, world experts have told us that it could last for only a couple of hundred years at the most. But there it is, right on that stone tool, which cannot be 13,000 years old! Of course, there's something obviously very wrong with evolutionary dating methods.

Genesis 1 is the true account of the origin of all people, including Aborigines!

Q. *Did Charles Darwin come up with the idea of evolution?*

A. Actually, no. All Darwin did was popularize a particular view of evolution. In fact, Darwin's grandfather was an evolutionist. And when we go further back in history, we find that the ancient Greeks — over 2,000 years ago — were evolutionists.

Perhaps the greatest lie Satan has convinced people of is that there's no God, and one of the chief ways he's done this is through promoting ideas like evolution.

When we go to Genesis and read the story about the serpent in the Garden of Eden, we find that the temptation given to Adam and Eve was that they could become as "gods." Think about it — this is a form of evolution, that we can evolve (if you like) into gods. Evolution is really a whole belief system that is anti-God, designed to explain all of life without the Creator. Therefore, this makes man his own god.

Satan has used evolution — even from the ancient times — to take people away from the truths we read about in Genesis. And it's happening more today than ever before!

Q. *Can rock layers such as the ones we see at the Grand Canyon actually form quickly?*

A. They certainly can. The story that you hear at the Grand Canyon is that it took millions of years of processes to lay down the material to form rock layers. But in some research that's been conducted at Mount St. Helens in Washington state, it's been shown that layers of rocks can be laid down very quickly.

At Mount St. Helens, there's one rock layer that's 30 feet thick. It was formed after a volcanic eruption in the early 1980s — but it took just one afternoon! Now the interesting thing is that this layer consists of thousands of individual layers, some only one millimeter thick. Normally this kind of rock layer would be interpreted — especially by evolutionists — as taking a long time to form.

What's the point? Well, creation scientists have been ridiculed by evolutionists for saying that the catastrophic events of Noah's flood formed most of the fossil layers over the earth — and very quickly. What happened at Mount St. Helens is just on a small scale, but it did show geologists that such layers can form quickly, just as the creationists have been claiming all along!

Q.
Are there real scientists who are
creationists?

A. I've met hundreds of real scientists who believe in the Genesis account of creation. In fact, most of the famous scientists who ever lived were creationists. Names like Michael Faraday, James Clerk Maxwell, Isaac Newton, Johannes Kepler, and so on, were some of the most famous scientists who ever lived. They believed in the God of creation, and they accepted Genesis as literal history.

I remember when I spoke to a number of scientists near Baltimore at the Goddard Space Center. It was a thrill to see many scientists, real scientists, who are involved in the space shuttle program, repairing the Hubble Telescope, and so on, who told me that they believed that Genesis is accurate and that evolution is wrong. There are thousands of scientists just like them throughout our world.

What should all scientists believe about where they came from? The answer's in Genesis — God created us, in His image.

Q. *When does a human being begin to exist?*

A. Abortionists say a number of things. Some declare that you can abort babies only up until about six months, or as a judge in Scotland ruled recently, a baby only becomes human when it's born. But this goes totally against what the Bible clearly says.

In Psalm 139 and Psalm 51, the Bible states that we begin as a human being right at the point of conception. So yes, abortionists are killing human beings regardless of how long the baby's been in the womb.

Also, our answers from Genesis tell us that God made man in His image. Thus, those who abort babies are killing humans who are made in the image of God.

Think about it — why has there been such an increase in abortion throughout the world? Largely, it's because so many people have been taught evolutionary ideas. They've been brainwashed to believe that what's in the womb is just an animal and therefore can be aborted.

We need to get our answers from God's Word, not man's opinions.

Q. *Is evolution fundamental to developing current technologies?*

A. I once received a phone call from a man who said he was a Christian. He was real upset with me because he'd heard me lecture against evolution. He declared, "Evolution binds all of science together," and that if scientists didn't believe it, they wouldn't be able to develop our technology today.

I asked him to give me just one example where evolution had helped to advance science. He said, "Medicine." So, I asked him for a specific instance. But first, I told him that I could give examples where evolution had actually caused medical research to go backwards. For instance, doctors once believed that our appendix was a useless leftover from our evolutionary ancestors.

Well, after hearing me he was stumped. He tried to shift gears and said that evolution had helped physics. I asked him again for one specific example where evolution had helped to build the space shuttle. Well, he couldn't.

The real reason scientists can develop our wonderful technologies today is because God created a real world with the laws of physics, which man can use for his good and God's glory.

Q. *Is the tailbone just a useless leftover from evolution?*

A. Unfortunately, some evolutionists call our tailbone a "vestigial" organ. This is a word often used by evolutionists to describe organs that they believe are useless leftovers from our evolutionary ancestry. They claim that they no longer have any function.

The appendix and the tonsils, for instance, were once considered vestigial organs. However, we know now that these organs have many important functions.

Now for the tailbone, which is not really a "bone in a tail" at all. Our tailbone is not vestigial — it has a very, very important function. If you've fallen down the stairs and landed on your tailbone, you'll find out just how important it is! It's quite necessary for muscles to be attached to it — those muscles that enable us to walk, sit down, and so on.

No, the tailbone is not vestigial. It was created for a specific purpose by the Creator. In fact, people who get their answers from Genesis can confidently state that there are no such things as useless, vestigial organs. Evolutionists are now finding out what the creationists have known all along.

Q. *Does evolution actually cause evils like abortion?*

A. No, but it's true that the increasing acceptance of abortion, homosexual activity, and so on have gone hand in hand as evolution has increased in popularity. Of course, that doesn't mean that every evolutionist is an abortionist, or every abortionist an evolutionist.

Now think about this: Why is a Christian against such things as abortion and homosexual behavior? It's because he believes that God is Creator, and thus He owns everything and everyone. Therefore, we're accountable to Him. This means that it is God who has a right to set the rules. And in God's Word, we read that life begins at conception, and that homosexual behavior is an abomination to the Lord.

But the more that people in society believe the Bible is not God's Word, and that we're just the animal products of evolution, isn't it logical that we will say that we're accountable to no one but ourselves? Therefore, we can decide our own rules about living.

So what's the cause of these social ills? The answer's in Genesis — sin!

Q. *Did cavemen really exist?*

A. Yes, they did. My definition is quite simple: cavemen are just men who live in caves.

Sadly, many people have the idea that a person who uses stone tools — and lives in a cave — is very primitive and nowhere near as advanced as we are. However, the Bible actually helps us understand who the cavemen were.

After Babel, different groups of people traveled in different directions all over the earth. There would have been an immediate loss of culture and technology. Until they found suitable materials, people would have used stone tools and, yes, perhaps lived in caves. But this didn't mean that they lost any of their intelligence or their human characteristics.

For example, in a burial chamber in Portugal, which was full of tools of stone and bone, scientists found what looked like a bone flute. Now this is puzzling to evolutionists because they'd never think that the "Stone Agers" had musical instruments.

Should we be surprised to find an ancient flute? The answer's in Genesis. Adam's descendants actually built musical instruments — look up Genesis 4:21.

Q. *Didn't creationists win the Scopes trial in 1925?*

A. Well, technically, the creationists were victorious. But it was a classic case of winning the battle but the beginnings of losing the war in America.

The ACLU lawyer, Clarence Darrow, was sly enough to write into the court record all of the so-called "scientific" evidence for evolution. He had many prominent scientists of the day present the best case for evolution. Interestingly, almost all of their so-called "facts" have been refuted today — in most instances by evolutionists themselves.

Darrow also was clever to have the Christian prosecutor, William Jennings Bryan, put on the witness stand. Unfortunately, Bryan couldn't answer Darrow's questions like, "Where did Cain get his wife?" and "Were the days of creation just ordinary 24-hour days?" Sadly, Bryan, a very fine and godly man, couldn't defend his faith.

All the media exposure at the Scopes trial helped lead to the decline of Christianity in America. Christians were seen as having just a "blind faith." In 1925 most Christians didn't have answers from Genesis — it's a lesson for all of us today.

Q. *How are dogs mutant disasters?*

A. Once I met with a veterinarian and told him that we had just obtained a small dog for our children. The vet, learning about the kind of dog we chose, looked at me and said, "Ken, I hope you realize what sort of a biological disaster you have there!"

I was kind of taken back and asked what he meant. "Well," he said, "the dog you have has all sorts of problems. You'll need to make sure it gets its injections, tablets, and have it groomed often. I make my living out of keeping these biological disasters alive!"

Here's what he was telling me. Domestic breeds of dogs have all sorts of mutations — mistakes in their genes because of the Curse. My vet friend said that he uses this information to speak against evolution to his customers. Unfortunately, many people think that when they see changes in dogs that this is some sort of upward evolutionary change. This is certainly not evidence of evolution. It's really just "variation" within the dog kind that God originally made in Genesis 1. Think about it: these dogs aren't improving at all. My dog may be cute, but it still has many mistakes in its genes resulting from the curse of Genesis 3.

Q. *Is it true that we are taller today, and isn't this evidence for evolution?*

A. Well, let's look at a practical study that was conducted on this very topic.

In my homeland of Australia, a survey was conducted a few years ago that showed that the average 10 year old was about an inch and a half taller and four pounds heavier than ten year olds had been 15 years before. It also found that the average 12-year-old girl today is about four inches taller and five pounds heavier than in 1911. What do the scientists say about this? They believe the major causes are better nutrition and fewer infectious diseases during childhood. It has nothing to do with evolution.

I've heard some people try to say that as man has evolved, he has become taller. However, one of the so-called "early humans," called *Homo erectus* was six feet tall. By the way, he was fully human and not halfway between ape and man.

Are people evolving when they get taller? No, that's another false idea. Evolutionists would know better if they would accept God at His Word, that He created the first man from dust.

Q: *How is the fossil record evidence of judgment?*

A. Across the earth, there are sedimentary layers up to miles thick, filled with billions of fossils. Now fossils, of course, are the preserved remains of animals and plants.

Evolutionists teach that the fossil record was formed over millions of years and thus represents millions of years of history.

However, the Bible makes it plain in Genesis that death, bloodshed, and suffering of animals and man entered the world only after Adam sinned. If this is true, then the billions of dead things in the layers of rocks had to be formed AFTER Adam rebelled.

Genesis 6–9 records the details of Noah's flood. This was a judgment on man's wickedness. If there really was a global flood, billions of animals would be buried in mud that would turn into rock. In other words, most of the fossil deposits are actually a record of this judgment — NOT a record of millions of years.

When we look at the fossil record, we should be reminded of the awfulness of sin, and the holiness of God who judged man's rebellion.

Q. *What's so revealing about* T-rex *fossil droppings?*

A. Many people might not get too thrilled about this — but scientists found a fossil *T-rex* dropping weighing about 15 pounds! Actually, scientists can learn a lot about an animal's eating habits by examining such fossils.

For instance, they found the ground-up bones of a plant-eating dinosaur in the *T-rex* coprolite. This means that this *T-rex* was feeding on other animals.

Now why is this revealing? Well, Genesis 1:29–30, tells us that before sin entered the world, all animals were vegetarian. There was no death, disease, or bloodshed before sin.

The implication for the Christian is that the fossil *T-rex* dropping could NOT be millions of years old as evolutionists claim. Why not? If all animals were vegetarian before sin, then this particular *T-rex* must have been eating animals sometime AFTER sin entered the world.

This is just another of the many reasons why Christians can't accept the belief that the fossil record was formed millions of years before man existed. Our answers in Genesis tell us that dinosaurs were created alongside of man on the sixth day of creation, just a few thousand years ago.

Q. *How do fossil bones relate to the gospel message?*

A. Well, let's think carefully about a fossil bone.

First of all, we can observe that the bone is dead — obviously! As Christians, we should be reminded of the Scripture that teaches us that the wages of sin is death. Thus, death is a reminder of sin — of our rebellion in Adam.

Second, we know that to form a fossil takes a catastrophic event — the animal must be buried quickly to be preserved. The Bible tells us of the event of Noah's flood — a judgment on man's wickedness. As a result of the flood, billions of animals were buried and eventually fossilized.

Third, as we think about the flood — we should also be reminded that God provided an ark of salvation for Noah and his family. This is also a picture of Jesus Christ — the Son of God who is our ark of salvation.

Because of sin, we were separated from God. However, Jesus Christ came to earth as a man to die and pay the penalty of sin. Just as Noah had to go through a doorway to be saved — so we must go through a doorway to be saved — and Jesus Christ is that door.

Q. *What lessons can fossils teach us?*

A. At a Christian school chapel where I was speaking recently, I held up a fossil dinosaur bone and asked the students to tell me everything they knew about this bone.

At first they were a little perplexed. After all, what can you say about a dead piece of bone?

I then preached a message using this fossil bone. The dead bone should remind us that death has entered the world because of sin — death is an intrusion, an enemy. This bone may have belonged to an animal that died during the flood of Noah's day. Thus, it is a reminder that God judges sin.

The Bible teaches us that just as there was a past judgment by water — so there is a coming final judgment, but next time by fire. And how can we be saved from this judgment to come? Just as Noah had to go through a doorway to be saved, so we need to go through a "door" — the Lord Jesus Christ — so we can be saved.

When we start from the Bible, knowing the history of the universe, we already have ANSWERS that we can use to explain the world around us.

Q. *What should fossils remind us of?*

A. After the miracle of the crossing of the Jordan River, Joshua instructed the Israelites to take 12 stones and build a memorial as a reminder of what God did for them. We read in the Bible that Joshua told the people that when their children ask the question, "What mean these stones?" — they were to be told of this wonderful miracle.

These 12 stones were to stand as a memorial for the children of future generations, so God's people wouldn't forget what God did.

This is a reminder to me that when our children look at the fossil record all over the earth, and ask us the question — "What mean these stones?" Our answer should be, "God judged sin with death — that's why we see death in the world today and in the fossil record."

Also, at the time of Noah, God judged the wickedness of man with a global flood. As a result of the flood, billions of fossils were formed all over the earth.

What mean these stones? Don't forget to tell your children the TRUTH about fossils!

Q. *What are polystrate fossils, and how are they a problem for evolution?*

A. Well, evolutionists believe that most of the layers of sedimentary rock on the earth's surface were laid down slowly over millions and millions of years. Most of these layers contain fossils of plants and animals.

Now here's the problem for evolutionists! There are a number of places on the earth where fossils actually penetrate more than one layer of rock. These are called "polystrate fossils."

For example, at the Joggins, in Nova Scotia, there are many erect fossil trees that are scattered throughout 2,500 feet of layers. You can actually see these fossil trees, which are beautifully preserved, penetrate through layers that were supposedly laid down over millions of years.

But the fact is, the trees had to be buried faster than it took them to decay. In other words, there's NO WAY these layers could have been laid down slowly over millions of years of supposed earth history. The trees would have rotted well before then and not fossilized.

Our answers in Genesis give a better explanation — Noah's flood, just thousands of years ago. This is just another of the MANY evidences consistent with the Bible's teaching of a young earth.

Q. *Is it true that fossils in the rock layers are — from bottom to top — consistent with evolution?*

A. It's true that there's a general order to the fossils — in the rock layers. However, there are many exceptions that make it clear that this is NOT evidence for evolution.

For instance, according to the evolutionary time scale, pine trees could not have appeared earlier than 350 million years ago. However, scientists have found fossil pine pollen in the Grand Canyon's Precambrian Hakatai shale.

Now the problem with this — as far as evolutionists are concerned — is that this shale is supposed to be at least 1.5 billion years old. According to evolutionary theory, this was WAY before any land life was supposed to appear. So how can you have pine pollen from pine trees appearing on earth hundreds of millions of years before pine trees even evolved? There's no way.

The true explanation comes from our answers in Genesis. Most of the fossil rock layers are the result of Noah's flood. This catastrophic event would not only have buried lots of animals and plants, it would have sorted them out as they were deposited. Evolution fails again!

Q. *Don't evolutionists believe that modern man evolved from primitive humans and that it began with a period called the Stone Age?*

A. Yes they do. And evolutionary scientists claim that this supposed Stone Age lasted for at least 100,000 years. They believe that Neanderthal man and Cro Magnon man lived at this time and that their population remained constant between one and ten million individuals.

Now we know that these people buried their dead with artifacts, such as stone axes. If you do a quick calculation, you'll find they should've buried at least four billion bodies.

According to evolutionists, they have bones that are supposedly much older than this. In other words, on the basis of their own theories, they should expect to find many of the bones of these billions of skeletons.

But here's something that is perplexing for the evolutionists. Only a few thousand such skeletons have been found. This implies that the Stone Age was much, much shorter than evolutionists think. In reality, it was only a few hundred years in some areas!

From our answers in Genesis, we'd expect people to use stone tools when they moved to new areas — there would've been many "stone ages" during the past few thousand years.

And these humans were not primitive!

Q. *Do geologists still believe that the Grand Canyon was eroded over millions of years by the Colorado River?*

A. Actually, many evolutionary geologists have now changed their minds about the formation of the Grand Canyon. They've come to recognize that the Colorado River could not have eroded the canyon in the supposed millions of years once believed for its formation.

Secular geologists have now come up with a new idea — they believe massive FLOODS over millions of years formed the Grand Canyon. Maybe the canyon's museum displays will now change!

Well, at least they're getting closer to what creationists have been saying all along. Creation scientists believe the various rock layers of the canyon were laid down during the flood and then uplifted towards the end of the flood. This explains why some of the rock layers are bent.

This uplift formed a dam, trapping some of the leftover water from the flood. This water then broke through the uplifted layers — forming the Grand Canyon.

There is much evidence consistent with this idea. You see, the Grand Canyon is NOT a testimony to millions of years of earth history — but a testimony to the judgment of the flood!

Q. *Have evolutionary scientists accurately reconstructed fossil records?*

A. A student approached me once with an illustrated book on evolution in his hand. He opened up to a picture of one of our supposed ancestors called "Lucy." Lucy looked somewhat human, but yet ape-like. The student asked me, "How do they know Lucy looked like this?" I replied that this was a good question. I explained that if someone were to dig up his own skull in a hundred years, they could find an artist to draw a picture and make him look ape-like or human-like. The student wondered, "Do scientists really just make up information?" I responded, "Actually, they sometimes do."

I shared with him a story about a medical illustrator who was contracted to produce drawings for a biology text. One of the drawings was to be of Lucy. When the illustrator finished his drawing, the book's authors rejected it, claiming it was too human-like. He was told to make Lucy look more ape-like.

Keep this story in mind the next time you read a book on evolution or visit a science museum. Ask yourself: Is this really imaginative art or science?

Q. *Why do so many of the fossils displayed in museums look exactly like creatures living today?*

A. Let me give you an example of how blind evolutionists can be to the obvious. Consider crayfish fossils. Their burrows have been found in rocks that have been supposedly dated at 220 million years old. But when the evolutionary scientists looked at them, they were surprised to discover that they were almost identical to modern crayfish.

Now there are two problems for evolutionists here. First, if the processes of evolution are still active, why is it that in 220 million supposed years, the crayfish haven't changed at all! Second, crayfish that die naturally don't automatically turn into fossils. They wouldn't be preserved unless some catastrophic burial occurred.

So what's the truth about these fossil crayfish? The answer's in Genesis: They represent the original created crayfish of Genesis 1 that were eventually buried by the flood of Genesis 6. The answer is simple when you reject evolution and accept the Bible.

The State
of the
World

Q: *If there's a God of love, why does He allow death and suffering?*

A. The answer is in Genesis! The only way we can understand how to reconcile our world of death and suffering with a loving God, is when the Book of Genesis is taken as literal history.

The Bible makes it plain that at the end of the sixth day of creation, God pronounced His creation as VERY GOOD. There was no death of animals or man — no suffering, no disease — it was a perfect world.

However, our ancestor, the first man Adam, rebelled against the Holy Creator God. Thus, Adam forfeited his right (and therefore the right of all his descendants — which includes us) to live in perfect harmony with God.

Because God is holy, pure, and without sin — He had to judge man's sin. Adam had been warned that death would be the penalty for rebellion. The death and suffering of this present world is a result of OUR sin! But we should also remember that God's Son became a Man to suffer this death and be resurrected, so those who trust in Christ can live forever with Him.

Q: Why shouldn't we blame God for death?

A. I believe that because much of the Church has been taught to believe in millions of years of earth's history, Christians often don't understand what death is all about.

You see, most people have been indoctrinated with the idea that the fossil record took millions of years to be laid down — that dinosaur bones are millions of years old, and so on.

Now when Christians believe this — and sadly, the majority probably do — then they've accepted that there were millions of years of death, suffering, and bloodshed before God made the first man.

Thus, they believe that God used the process of death and suffering over millions of years as part of the process of creation. So, when a loved one dies, it would be logical for these people to blame God for death.

However, Genesis makes it plain that death entered the world AFTER Adam sinned — it was a judgment BECAUSE of sin. The Bible describes death as an ENEMY. When a loved one dies, we should fall on our knees before our Holy God recognizing that death is in the world because WE sinned.

146 ~ Death & Disease

Q: How does death show that God is a God of love?

A. When the first man Adam rebelled against God, he forfeited his right to live with a Holy God. In fact, God had warned Adam that if he disobeyed the commandment not to eat the fruit of the Tree of Knowledge and Evil, he'd have to die.

Because Adam was the head of the human race, then all of his descendants fell with him when he rebelled. Thus, we're all under the judgment of death because of sin. Because we're made in God's image, even though our body dies, we'll still live forever. As sinners, we'd be separated from God forever. To live with God, the penalty for sin would have to be paid.

However, God loved us so much, that He planned before the creation to provide a way for the payment for sin. In judging man with death, God knew that He would send His Son to become a man — but a perfect man — so He could suffer death. God then raised Him from the dead, accepting Christ's death as payment for sin.

Think about it! Without death — we couldn't be redeemed!

Q. *What has death got to do with the creation-evolution debate?*

A. There are many Christians who accept the teachings of evolution yet state that God used this method in creating life on this planet. Thus, they see nothing wrong with believing that God used the evolutionary processes to produce plants and animals . . . and eventually man.

However, Christians who think this way need to realize that there are many insurmountable problems in trying to reconcile evolution with the account of origins in Genesis.

Our answers in Genesis make it plain that there was no death of animals or man before sin. In fact, Genesis 1 states that originally, before sin, all the animals and Adam and Eve were vegetarian. It was a perfect world, described as **VERY GOOD.**

However, the processes of evolution involve death, bloodshed, violence, and suffering over millions of years before man arrived on the scene.

Christians can't reconcile the Bible's account of a perfect world that had no bloodshed and death with a view that teaches death and bloodshed existed right from the start!

God, who knows everything, tells us in Genesis that death resulted from sin.

Q. Will there be death in the new heaven and earth?

A. The Book of Revelation declares that in the new heaven and earth there will be no death, crying, or suffering. It will be a perfect place.

Now the reason I asked the question about death was to point out an inconsistency in many Christians' thinking. You see, I've found that the majority of Christians think they have to accept that the fossil record is millions of years old. Thus, they accept that death, disease, bloodshed, and suffering existed from the beginning.

However, Genesis makes it plain that death entered the world AFTER sin. Now here's another important point. One day in the future, God is going to restore this creation — in other words, He is going to make it just like it was before sin.

Now if death, bloodshed, disease, and suffering existed before sin — then the restitution must be like this, also! No, the new creation will be perfect, without death — just as it was before sin.

The belief in millions of years of history destroys the teachings of the new heaven and earth, and actually undermines the gospel.

Q. *What will the future state in heaven be like?*

A. In Isaiah, I believe we're given a picture of what the future state will be like. We're told that the wolf will dwell with the lamb and that the lion will eat straw like an ox.

Now this is a very different picture to today's world where we could say that the lamb dwells IN the wolf! In other words, the world today is one of death and struggle. It's a groaning, suffering world.

However, in the future state, animals that eat each other today will be living peaceably together. Instead of being meat-eaters — they will be vegetarian.

Actually, this future state, which the Bible describes as a RESTORATION, is the same as the perfect world before sin. God tells us in Genesis that animals and Adam and Eve were only to eat plants and fruits originally. There was no death or bloodshed in the world.

Sadly, when Christians believe in millions of years of death before Adam, they've destroyed this teaching of the restoration. Christians can't accept millions of years — this destroys the answers in Genesis concerning sin and death.

Q: *How is evolution a religion and not science?*

A. Not only is evolution a belief system, but it's a horrible religion of death!

You see, a religion can be defined as a concept, or principle or system of belief, held to with ardor and faith. This is exactly what evolution is.

When I was a teacher in Australia, I taught my students real science. They used their five senses in the present to investigate the world. This is the kind of science that put man on the moon. However, evolution is a belief about the past — and we can't directly investigate the past. For example, we can't see reptiles evolving into birds — that's the evolutionists' belief or religion.

But it's also a religion of death. Evolution teaches that death existed from the beginning. The deaths of billions of creatures over billions of years finally led to man. When a person dies — that's the end of them. Death saves us from living.

But our answers from Genesis tell us that death is an intrusion . . . because of sin. When we die, we live forever — with God or without Him. That's why Jesus Christ came to die — so we might live forever with Him!

Q. *How was the tree of the knowledge of good and evil a tree of death?*

A. When God made Adam, He didn't create him to be a puppet. He wanted Adam to love and obey Him. God told Adam he could eat of any tree in the Garden — but there was ONLY ONE tree he was not to eat of. If he disobeyed, then he would have to die.

God also planted a special tree called the "tree of life." Now I call this tree of the knowledge of good and evil the "tree of death." This is because if Adam ate from it, then death would enter the world.

In a real sense, Adam had a choice — the tree of life or the tree of death. Sadly, he chose the tree of death. That's why there is death all around us. It is a judgment from a Holy God because of sin.

However, our answers in Genesis tell us that through death God would provide a way for man to come back to a perfect relationship with his Creator!

Q. Can a God that uses evolution be a God of love?

A. Think about the thousands of students each year who are indoctrinated in our education systems not to believe God's Word. By and large, they're taught that evolution is fact, and that through millions of years of death, disease, and suffering, man evolved.

Now if you take these students and tell them there's a God of love — how would they react? From my experience, many will say something like, "How can there be a God of love when you see all this death and suffering in the world? We see little children dying — people starving — people crying out in pain from horrible diseases — there can't be a God of love."

You see, the problem is that these students are looking at a groaning world — it's because of sin. However, because they've been indoctrinated not to believe in sin, they don't understand how one can reconcile a God of love with this hurting world.

It's only when these students are shown that evolution is a lie, and the answers in Genesis are true, that they will begin to understand that God truly is a God of love.

Q. *Why would any man carry out such terrible acts as murdering and then cannibalizing his victims as Jeffrey Dahmer did?*

A. According to his own words, Dahmer was simply applying what he'd been taught about evolution.

Listen to what he said on NBC television:

> If a person doesn't think there is a God to be accountable to, then what's the point of trying to modify your behavior to keep it within acceptable range? That's how I thought, anyway. I always believed the theory of evolution is truth, that we all just came from slime. When we died, you know, that was it, there's nothing.

It is not surprising that when you take generations of children and train them in a public educational system that they're just animals, then why shouldn't they act like animals?

Even though we can't know for sure whether or not he trusted Christ in his last days, the answer to horrible crimes like murder can be found in Dahmer's own words. He said "I, as everyone else, will be accountable to Him," meaning his Creator.

Q. Why would someone deny that the Creator is a very loving God?

A. If you just look at the world without the Bible, you actually see a horrible world. There are terrible diseases like cancer — children starving and dying — horrible accidents — murders — violent acts of terrorism. It's not a beautiful world.

Because most people have been indoctrinated to believe that the death and struggle we see around us today has gone on for millions of years of earth's history — you can understand why someone would say that there can't be a God of love.

However, the Bible tells us that the world was perfect at the start, with no death, disease, or violence. Animals and man were in perfect harmony. However, sin changed all that. Paul explains in Romans 8 that we live in a groaning world because of sin.

When Christians believe in millions of years, they really can't explain a God of love to a non-Christian. It's only the Christian who believes in a literal Genesis who can explain the origin of death because of OUR sin — and then they can share the truth of the loving God who sent His Son to redeem us.

Q. *Are there really white people in the world today?*

A. To be technically correct, no. Most people don't know that all human beings actually have the same skin color. Let me explain: We all have a pigment called "melanin." If you have a lot of melanin, you can be very dark, even black. Other than albinos, who don't have much pigment, no one is really white. We all have this brownish pigment. And it can be shown from simple genetics that if we started with Adam and Eve as middle-brown, that in just one generation there could be children who are black or light brown or anything in-between!

Now why do we have some groups of people in our world who are black, dark brown, and others middle-brown, and so on? The answer is in Genesis. After the event of the Tower of Babel, populations were split into groups, which resulted in certain shades of melanin being concentrated in particular groups. This is what we would call "natural selection" according to the creation model, not Darwin's theory.

This is another great example to help us understand that all human beings are descendants of the first couple, Adam and Eve.

Q. *Did God create different races of people in the beginning?*

A. No. The Bible clearly teaches in Corinthians that Adam was the first man. We're also told in Genesis that Eve was the mother of all the living.

But there are other reasons why it's clear — from the Bible — that Adam was the first and only human being at the beginning. We read in Genesis that Adam looked at all the creatures that God had made and he saw none that could be a mate for him. We're also told in Genesis that Adam was alone. Obviously, he wouldn't have been alone if there were other races of people around.

Also, keep this important point in mind: we inherit our sin nature from our first father, Adam. If there were other races of people that God supposedly made, and these people didn't sin as Adam did, and then Adam's sinful descendants married them, well, the whole gospel message then becomes meaningless.

Was Adam alone? The answer's in Genesis: God made one man, Adam, the father of the entire human race.

Q. *Are there at least four races of people?*

A. First of all, let me read a quote from a scientist at the American Association for the Advancement of Science convention in Atlanta.

Race is a social construct derived mainly from perceptions conditioned by events of recorded history, and it has no basic biological reality.

What this person is saying is that biologically, there is only ONE race of human beings. After all, all humans are classified as *Homo sapiens sapiens.*

Now if people had believed the Bible, beginning with Genesis, they would already know this. God's Word teaches us that ALL people are descendants of the same one man and one woman — Adam and Eve. As Paul says in Acts 17 — we are all of ONE BLOOD.

Evolutionists, though, have taught that there are different races of people. Darwin believed that different races evolved at different times. Sadly, this has resulted in many racial prejudices.

If everyone accepted the true history of mankind from Genesis, it would go a long way toward solving the problems of racism in today's world.

Q. *How many different skin colors are there among humans?*

A. Well, this may come as a shock to some people, but humans really only have one skin color!

All humans (except albinos) have a pigment in their skin called melanin. There are two forms of this pigment that give skin its color. People who are black have a lot of melanin. Those who are light have only a little of this pigment. Actually, the majority of people in the world are middle brown.

Assuming there were four genes for the amount of melanin in our skin, then it would make sense that Adam and Eve were middle brown. The possible combination of genes from such parents could result in children ranging from black to very light — in one generation! There are many families like this in the world today.

Because of the split-up of the gene pool at the time of the Tower of Babel, different combinations of genes ended up in the various people groups resulting in the pigment distribution we see in various cultures today. The evidence fits with the Bible's account of history.

Q: *Are there such things as "black" and "white" skin colors?*

A. Most people don't realize that all human beings are the same basic color. We all have the same skin pigment called melanin. It's just a matter of how much or how little we have. This pigment is produced by cells called melanocytes.

Dr. Anthony du Viver at London's King's College, made this statement:

> There are the same number of melano-cytes to be found in both Negroid and Caucasian skin.

If this is so, then why is Caucasian skin light and negroid black? Well the only difference is that the tiny pigment packaging units called "melanosomes" are slightly larger and more numerous per cell in dark-skinned than light-skinned people.

Many people think that skin color is a major difference among humans — but it's not. It's just a minor variation due to the amount of pigment. This fits with the fact that all humans are descendants of one man and one woman — Adam and Eve. We're all related — which is why we can preach the gospel to all people groups in the world — just as the Bible tells us to.

Q. *How could black parents have white children?*

A. Here's a real-life example that illustrates that the differences among humans really are only skin deep, so to speak.

A family in London, England, will be going in the *Guinness Book of Records.* And the reason? Well, both parents are of typical African appearance with dark skin, eyes, and hair. Yet their three children have white skin, blond hair, and hazel-green eyes!

The reason for this is because each child happened to inherit a gene for a form of albinism from each parent. This resulted in a very low production of the pigment melanin that is found in the skin, hair, and eyes.

The parents said that they had experienced some racist attitudes from people who thought these children couldn't be their own. This is because so many people don't understand that everyone has the same skin color and all belong to one race.

Because so many people have been brainwashed in evolutionary ideas, they incorrectly believe there are different races of people in the world. That's why we all need to get back to the correct biblical view of history — all humans are of one blood — descended from Adam.

Q. *How major are the racial differences among humans?*

A. In reality, what are called the "racial differences" are really quite insignificant.

When people talk about racial differences, they mean such things as skin color, eye shape, and so on. However, what most people don't realize is that these differences are very minor.

As we know, every person (except for identical twins) looks different to every other human being on the planet. We all have a unique combination of information in our genes. The difference genetically between any two persons is less than 1 percent — about .2 percent.

However, the so-called racial differences like skin color and eye shape constitute only .012 percent genetically. In other words, they are extremely insignificant.

In many instances, the reason we think these supposed racial differences are major is because we've been trained to think that way — usually because of evolutionary indoctrination. You see, evolutionists have taught us that humans are divided into four basic races — Negroid, Caucasoid, Mongoloid, and Australoid.

However, humans should be divided up on the basis of culture — not so-called race. There is only one race of humans because we are all descendants of one man, Adam.

Q. *How could we even know what color skin Adam and Eve had?*

A. Well first of all, everyone has the same color of skin. It is due to a pigment called melanin. If you have a lot of melanin, you would have very dark skin, whereas a little amount of melanin would result in light skin.

Now if we assume there are four genes for the amount of pigment in our skin — represented by capital A and B and small a and b — then we can work out the probable shade of Adam and Eve's skin.

Think through this with me: If Adam and Eve had all capital A's and B's for melanin — this would mean they would have been very dark and all their children would be dark. If they had small a's and b's for melanin — they and their children would have been very light.

However, if Adam and Eve had both capital and small a and b — then they would be middle brown in color. Their children then could have been a range of shades from dark to light. This is same range we see in the world today. So it makes sense genetically that Adam and Eve were middle brown in skin shade.

Q. *Does the question about where Cain got his wife really matter?*

A. Actually, this is a VERY important question. The Bible teaches us that ALL human beings are descendants of Adam and Eve. This is vital to an understanding of the gospel.

You see, the Lord Jesus Christ became a man — a descendant of Adam. He actually became our "relation" so He could die for all His relations. This is why all humans can have their sins forgiven if they repent and trust the Lord Jesus Christ.

Because Jesus became a man, only descendants of Adam can be saved. So you see — it's important to be able to defend that all human beings are descendants of the same one man and one woman.

So who was Cain's wife? Genesis 5:4 also states that Adam and Eve had sons and daughters. Cain must have married his sister. Now marrying a close relative wasn't a problem at the beginning — it was only outlawed at the time of Moses, when close relatives marrying often led to genetic mistakes in their offspring.

Q. *What are "pre-adamites?"*

A. Christians who accept man's fallible methods of dating objects as absolute have a real problem. You see, these dating methods are based on fallible assumptions, and wrongly date human skeletons back nearly 2 million years.

Now the Bible lists genealogies to show that Jesus Christ became a descendant of the first man, Adam. A strict chronology of the Bible places the creation of Adam about 6,000 years ago. There is no way that millions of years could be added into these genealogies — it would destroy them.

So what do Christians do with these human skeletons that supposedly date back hundreds of thousands or millions of years? Well they believe God MUST HAVE created humans without souls before Adam and Eve. A number of famous Christian leaders believe this. They say that God made Adam and Eve about 25,000 years ago after these supposed "soulless" humans (who did cave paintings and buried their dead) died out.

But these same dating methods indicate that the Australian Aborigines and American Indians supposedly lived 40,000 to 60,000 years ago. This would mean they couldn't be descendants of Adam and Eve. This also means they couldn't have salvation through Christ!

Can you see what shocking distortions occur when people try to marry man's theories to the Bible?

Q. *Many Christians claim that Ham was cursed because of what he did to his father, Noah. What does this have to do with skin color?*

A. Sadly, I've heard many Christians say that the curse of Ham resulted in people with black skin. Some religions, including the Mormons, used to teach this.

However, if one reads the Bible carefully, we find that Ham was NOT cursed. It was his son Canaan. And this had nothing whatsoever to do with black skin. For a start, everyone has the same color skin — it's just a matter of how much or how little of the pigment melanin we have in our skin.

Second, most of the descendants of Canaan were wiped out. Such people included the inhabitants of Sodom and Gomorrah.

Personally, I think the reason Canaan was cursed was because Noah saw in his grandson the same disrespectful and rebellious attitude he saw in his son Ham — only it was much worse. Noah knew what sort of people Canaan's descendants would be.

This should be a warning to all of us, particularly fathers, to train our children in the ways of the Lord so they won't be like Canaan.

Q. *How did the different people groups form?*

A. To answer this question, let's first of all think about how we obtained our domestic varieties of dogs. We know that all dogs are the same kind — but there are tremendous variations within the dog kind. This variability is inbuilt in the genes of the dogs — created by God when He made the dog kind.

As each dog is born, it has a unique combination of information that makes it a little different from every other dog — but it's still a dog. What we do is select certain dogs to breed together so we can concentrate particular genes together in one group. Thus, we end up with different breeds of dogs.

Now with the human population — to get the various groups with the people features that characterize a particular group — we would need to split up the human population and isolate particular groups.

The Bible tells us how this separation of groups happened — the Tower of Babel. It's the Bible's account of origins that makes sense of the world.

Q. *What does evolution have to do with racism? Didn't people have racist attitudes even before Darwin?*

A. It's certainly true that when people don't build their thinking on the Bible, they can end up with incorrect attitudes and thinking. Yes, there were certainly people with racist attitudes toward certain cultures before Darwin — but it's a fact of history that Darwinian evolution fueled racism.

The ardent evolutionist Stephen Jay Gould stated in one of his books, "Biological arguments for racism may have been common before 1850, but they increased by orders of magnitude following the acceptance of evolutionary theory."*

The point is, evolution inherently is a racist philosophy. It teaches that certain groups of people evolved at different times. Thus, some people groups would be closer to the apes.

Because of Darwinian evolution, many people in Darwin's time treated certain native peoples as just animals. In 1907 the well-respected *Scientific American* printed an article that stated the Congo pygmies were ape-like.

Sadly, many of these racist attitudes that were built on evolution persist to this day. The Bible though, beginning with Genesis, teaches that all humans are equal!

* Stphen Jay Gould, *Ontogeny and Phylogeny* (Cambridge, MA: Belknap-Harvard Press, 1977), p. 127–128.

Q. Were Australian Aborigines actually slaughtered as specimens for evolution?

A. It's a sad fact of history — but that's exactly what did happen!

Darwin believed that the Australian Aborigines were the "missing links" of evolution. As a result, hunters came to Australia to kill the Aborigines and bring them home as specimens for museums. In fact, in the early 1900s, the Aborigines were listed as animals in an Australian museum booklet!

There are many accounts of how various people hunted down Aboriginal men, women, and children. They were killed like animals — then skinned — and their skulls boiled down so the best specimens could be sent to places like America, England, and Germany.

It's been estimated that perhaps 10,000 bodies of Australian Aboriginal people were shipped to British museums in a frenzied attempt to prove the widespread belief that they were the missing link. American evolutionists were also involved in gathering specimens of so-called "sub humans." The Smithsonian Institution in Washington D.C. holds the remains of 15,000 individuals of various "races."

No wonder many people today still have racist attitudes — particularly when you realize that evolution is taught as fact throughout government education systems.

Q. *Why would anyone dig up someone's grave in the name of evolution?*

A. It's a well-known fact of history that Darwin believed the Australian Aborigines were the missing links between humans and apes. But there's even more to the story.

When the first English governor came to Australia in 1788, he took a couple of Aborigines back to England. When these Aborigines arrived in England, an English newspaper reported this event this way:

> They appear to be a race totally incapable of civilisation . . . they are from a lower order of the human race.

When one of these Aborigines eventually died, his body was dug up from its grave and stolen by Charles Darwin's grandfather to be stuffed and exhibited at the Royal College of Surgeons.

You see, Charles Darwin's grandfather was also an evolutionist — and he obviously influenced his grandson with evolutionary ideas. No wonder Charles Darwin had such racist attitudes towards the Aborigines!

Time and time again, the teaching of evolution has resulted in evil fruits. Remember, Hitler used evolution to justify his racist attitudes to the Jews. It's so important to tell people the truth about human origins — WE ARE all ONE race descended from our father Adam — who was made directly by our Creator God.

Q. *How is evolution responsible for a Pygmy in a zoo?*

A. This is a sad fact of American history. In 1904, a noted African explorer brought a Pygmy named Ota Benga to America from the Belgian Congo.

He was sent to the Bronx Zoo, where he was put on display in the monkey house. Records indicate that the zoo director saw no difference between a "wild beast and the little black man."

Evidence shows that both the zoo director and the explorer had been influenced by Darwinian evolution and its teaching that humankind could be divided into different races.

In the Pygmy's cage, the zoo officials also put an orangutan. Thousands of Americans came to the zoo to see this bizarre exhibit. There's no doubt that many people believed that this Pygmy was closely related to the orangutan. One account about Benga stated that he "was not much taller than the orangutan ... their heads are much alike, and both grin in the same way when pleased."*

This racism was just another shocking example of the evil fruits of evolution. This kind of situation wouldn't have occurred had people believed the truth of God's Word — that all humans are of one race.

* P.V. Bradford and H. Blume, *Ota Benga; The Pygmy in the Zoo* (St. Martins, 1992) p. 181.

Q. *What was Hitler's justification for killing millions of people — particularly Jews?*

A. To answer that question, let's look at a quote from a famous evolutionist, Sir Arthur Keith. He once wrote:

> To see evolutionary measures and tribal morality being applied rigorously to the affairs of a great modern nation, we must turn again to Germany of 1942. We see Hitler devoutly convinced that evolution produces the only real basis for a national policy. . . . The German Fuhrer, as I have consistently maintained, is an evolutionist; he has consciously sought to make the practices of Germany conform to the theory of evolution.

Because Hitler believed in evolution, he applied this practically in the culture. He set up the machinery to help nature eliminate those he believed were the unfit. First, those considered the "genetically inferior" — the mentally and physically disabled. Next, gypsies, Jews, and others.

Hitler developed his own form of racism based on his acceptance of evolutionary theory. Now just because someone believes in evolution DOES NOT necessarily mean THEY WILL be racist. But because evolution is a belief and not science, it can be used to justify any evil position — just as Hitler did.

Q. *If all people in the world today are descendants of just two parents, why do billions of people look so different from each other?*

A. Well, we all get one set of genes from our father and another from our mother. This results in a combination that's different from our parents — yet all the information in our genes comes from our parents.

Let me give you an idea of how much variability is found in our genes. If we were to take just two people — a man and woman — then, if it were possible, they could actually have more children than there are atoms in the known universe without two looking the same. That's an incredible amount of variability.

Think about this — there are estimated to be 10 to the 80th power atoms in the universe. However, the possible different combinations of genes from just two people is more than 10 to the 2000th power!

You know what else? God put this same sort of variability into the genes of animals. That's why we see a lot of variation — but this has NOTHING to do with evolution as Darwin thought. People remain people and dogs remain dogs — just as the Bible says in Genesis.

Q. *Do evolutionists now believe all people are descended from one woman?*

A. Some fascinating research certainly indicates this is so. Now evolutionists don't believe there was only one woman to start with — but some do believe that all humans today are descendants of one particular woman.

In the cytoplasm of our cells are organelles called "mito-chondria." These structures also contain some DNA that is ONLY inherited from the woman. In analyzing this DNA in humans all over the globe, scientists showed that all humans on earth inherited this from one woman.

At first, this research indicated that the woman whose mitochondrial DNA was ancestral to that in all living people — lived about 100,000 to 200,000 years ago. However, later research on the mutation rate also resulted in another startling conclusion — this woman had to live about 6,000 years ago. This fits beautifully with the time line of history as recorded in God's Word.

Evolutionists are not suddenly re-reading the Bible's account of the creation of the first man and woman. However, this is just another example of how real science supports what the Bible has stated all along!

Q. *Does the Bible say anything about interracial marriage?*

A. First of all, we need to understand that there is only ONE race of humans. For instance, the ABC-TV news science department had an article that stated, "More and more scientists find that the differences that set us apart are cultural, not racial. Some even say that the word race should be abandoned because it's meaningless."

This of course agrees with the Bible's account of history — we're all of ONE blood, descended from Adam. There are no different races. This also means that in reality there is no such thing as interracial marriage!

The Bible makes it clear that the priority in marriage is to make sure your mate is a Christian so that you are not unequally yoked. Remember Rahab the Canaanite and Ruth the Moabite? They trusted in the real God and became Israelites. The important thing is that the husband and wife trust in the true God.

Now it is true that if you marry someone from a totally different culture, you need to be warned that you may have communication difficulties because of the cultural differences — but there's nothing in the Bible against so-called "interracial marriage."

Q. *Surely these days evolutionists wouldn't teach the same kinds of racist ideas that Darwin wrote about 150 years ago, would they?*

A. It's certainly true that Darwin was a racist. He believed that humankind was divided into different races — and that certain races were more primitive or "ape-like" than others. There's no doubt this led to many racist attitudes toward certain people groups over the years.

It's been said that Darwin's *Origin of Species,* published in 1859, is second to the Bible in influencing the way people think about life. The full title of Darwin's book is as follows:

> *On the Origin of Species by Means of Natural Selection or the Preservation of Favoured Races in the Struggle for Life*

Something most people are not aware of is that evolution still is inherently a racist philosophy. Most evolutionists try to hide this — but it's true, nonetheless. For instance, in a book by a Canadian professor entitled *Race, Evolution and Behavior*, he actually ranks the so-called races along an evolutionary scale with blacks at the bottom and Asians at the top.

He is being honest about the real nature of evolution. It's only the Bible that teaches the truth about humans — WE ARE all one race, descendants of Adam.

Q. *Did humans evolve at different times?*

A. Let's think about this carefully. I'm going to list four combinations of people in marriage, and I want you to consider which one God would be against — according to the Bible:

> First – A Christian man with almond-shaped eyes and a Christian woman with Caucasian eyes.
>
> Second – A non-Christian man and a non-Christian woman.
>
> Third – A Christian man with dark skin and a Christian woman with light skin.
>
> Fourth – A non-Christian Caucasian man with a Christian Caucasian woman.

From a biblical perspective, it's number four. The only one of those marriages that God speaks against in the Bible is the Christian marrying the non-Christian. This is what I call true interracial marriage — it's when a child of the last Adam marries a child of the first Adam.

Sadly, because so many Christians have been indoctrinated by evolutionary ideas, they think humankind is divided into different races. More people end up concerned about people from so-called different races marrying rather than whether or not they are equally yoked spiritually — which IS the most important thing in marriage!

Q. Why should the term "races" be dropped?

A. At the time of Thomas Jefferson, 200 years ago, when people used the term "races" they would think of the Irish race or English race and so on. However, Charles Darwin changed all that when he published his book *On the Origin of Species*. The title actually included the words "*the Preservation of Favored Races in the Struggle for Life.*"

Darwin was a racist. He believed that different groups of people evolved at different times, and so some cultures were more like apes than others. Sadly, this fueled racist attitudes toward different people groups.

Because of this, the word "races" today still conjures up evolutionary overtones. Many people think "evolution" when they hear this word.

As a result of this situation, I believe we need to drop the term "races" when talking about mankind. Based on the Bible, and understanding the split-up of people due to the Tower of Babel event, I believe we should use the term "people groups." After all — there is only ONE race of people, all descendants of Adam.

Q. *What's the solution to racism?*

A. Personally, I believe the solution is quite simple. First of all, let me explain that more and more secular scientists are realizing that there is only one race of people. The so-called "racial differences" are extremely minor. Sadly, evolution has indoctrinated people to believe that different races of people evolved at different times. This has led to many racist attitudes towards certain cultures.

An anthropologist recently stated:

> If it is determined that races do not bio-
> logically exist, or even if they do that one
> is not biologically superior to others,
> communication of these findings to the
> populous may help to solve the problems
> associated with racism.

The only view that communicates this situation clearly is the biblical one. The Bible teaches that ALL people are equal before God, because all are descendants of one man, Adam. All humans are of one race — and all suffer from sin. Thus, all people need to trust Jesus Christ as Savior and build their entire thinking on God's Word. If people accepted this — there would be no racism.

Q. *What has evolution got to do with the recent, terrible problem of school violence?*

A. People have been shocked in recent times at the outbreaks of school violence in America. Some schools are now using metal detectors and other security measures to try to curb such violent behavior.

So, what has evolution got to do with this sad and shocking situation?

I believe what we see happening is the outworking of an education system that has eliminated God from the classroom. When you think about it, generations of young people are being brainwashed each day in evolutionary ideas. They're being told that they're nothing special — they're just animals that have evolved from some lower form of animal over millions of years.

The more the culture as a whole thinks this way, the more society will act consistently with what they've been taught. If life's not special — then it has no value. If there's no God, and thus no absolute authority, then anyone can decide right and wrong for themselves.

I don't think the students actually realize the connection of violence with evolution — but underneath it all, this anti-God religion has subtly caused them to think in this vein of hopelessness and purposelessness.

Q. *Is it true that one of America's humanist groups is actually targeting children, families, and college students with anti-God propaganda?*

A. Yes — and Christians need to be made aware of this. In one of the leading humanist organization's newsletters, they stated: "Our unprecedented college and university outreach has sparked formation of atheist and humanist groups on more than 70 campuses. More than 200 new groups are in the process of forming."

Also in the same letter, they explain how they're targeting families:

> You've seen *Family Matters*, our new publication for parents who've taken on the challenge of raising humanist children in a culture obsessed with faith. Our moral education program for children has gone through two years of development here (and) we plan to launch a regular program of critical-thinking classes for the young, which could go nationwide as early as 1999.

The humanists are on the march to eliminate God from the culture. One of the most successful ways they're accomplishing this is through the teaching of evolution in schools and colleges. Help us to spread the truth of the answers in Genesis that can help save this nation from moral collapse!

Q: *Should Christians try to force the teaching of creation in schools?*

A. Frankly, we really need to think this one through carefully.

First of all, many non-Christian teachers accept evolution as fact. They wouldn't do justice to the teaching of creation. No matter how good a creation scientist's research might be in certain areas, it'll be omitted by the teacher.

Here is what I would like to see. Science needs to be taught correctly in our schools. If students know what science really is and if they're taught the correct definition of science, they'll understand that evolution is not a fact. You see, science is working in the present, conducting experiments, coming up with fabulous technologies, and so on. Evolution, though, is just a belief system about the past. You don't see it happening today, and you can't go back into the past to show how it happened. Evolution is not science.

We should teach real science in our government schools, and Christians need to help build an educational system that will do it.

Q: *What should we teach our children about dating and marriage?*

A. All of our doctrines, like marriage, are founded in Genesis. Therefore, when we think about marriage — and dating, of course, would be a part of this — we should see what Genesis might say about this topic.

First, I've got to be truthful and say that I'm actually shocked at the number of Christian homes I've visited where I find that the sons and daughters are allowed to date just anybody. If I ask a question such as "Well, is he or she a Christian?" they look at me puzzled, as if to say, "Well, what's that got to do with it?"

Frankly, everything, if you understand marriage. According to the Bible, the primary importance of marriage is to produce godly offspring. The Bible also teaches that we're not to be unequally yoked.

You see, if we get our answers from Genesis and look at the doctrine of marriage, and realize that it's one man and one woman for life, who are to produce godly children, then we must come to the conclusion that Christians shouldn't date non-Christians. If we're all honest, we can think of many families who've been destroyed because Christians didn't obey this key principle. We must teach our children answers from Genesis!

Q. *Can we really know for sure if Adam and Eve had bellybuttons — and why would it matter anyway?*

A. Actually, I believe we can know, and it may surprise you that it's NOT just a trivial question.

The Bible teaches plainly that all human beings are descendants of one man — Adam. Paul tells us in Corinthians that Adam was the FIRST man.

How does the topic of bellybuttons relate to this? Well, Adam and Eve were not born of a woman as all other human beings must be. Adam was created directly from dust, and Eve from Adam's side.

Now a bellybutton is actually the scar of where a person was once connected by the umbilical cord to their mother. Adam and Eve would not have had such a scar because they were made as mature human beings — they weren't ever connected by an umbilical cord.

As I often like to say, when Adam and Eve told their descendants that they were the first two people, maybe they would have been asked, "How can you prove that?" All Adam and Eve would have to do is show them their bare tummies and say, "Look, no bellybutton!"

Resources

The text of this book was adapted from *Answers . . . with Ken Ham* radio scripts aired between November 23, 1998, and July 30, 1999.

For more information on any of the topics covered in this book, please review the following resource list or contact the AiG ministry nearest you (see last page).

The Garden of Eden and the Fall

The Genesis Record – Henry Morris (Grand Rapids, MI: Baker Book House, Co., 1979)

The Revised Answers Book – Don Batten, editor; Ken Ham; Jonathan Sarfati; Carl Wieland (Green Forest, AR: Master Books, Inc., 2000)

"Where Did Cain Get His Wife?" – Ken Ham, booklet (Answers in Genesis)

The Flood of Noah

The Revised Answers Book – Batten, editor, et al.

Noah's Ark: A Feasibility Study – John Woodmorappe (El Cajon, CA: Institute for Creation Research, 1996)

The World that Perished – John C. Whitcomb (Grand Rapids, MI: Baker Book House, Co., 1988)

Amazing Bible Facts about Noah's Ark – Ken Ham and Mark Dinsmore (Groton, VT: Wellspring Books)

Raging Waters — video (Answers in Genesis)

Mount St. Helens — video (Institute for Creation Research)

Dinosaurs

The Great Dinosaur Mystery Solved – Ken Ham
(Green Forest, AR: Master Books, Inc., 1998)
"Dinosaurs and the Bible" – Ken Ham, booklet
(Answers in Genesis)

Creation Evangelism

Creation Evangelism for the New Millennium –
Ken Ham (Green Forest, AR: Master Books,
Inc., 1999)
"Is There Really a God?" – Ken Ham, booklet
(Answers in Genesis)

The Gap Theory and Other Compromises

The Revised Answers Book – Batten, et al.
The Genesis Record – Morris
Unformed and Unfilled – Weston W. Fields
(Collinsville, IL: Burgener Enterprises, 1976)

Evidence for Creation

Creation: Facts of Life – Gary Parker (Green Forest,
AR: Master Books, Inc., 1994)
The Revised Answers Book – Batten, et al.
Stones and Bones – Carl Wieland (Green Forest, AR:
Master Books, Inc., 1996)
From a Frog to a Prince — video (Answers in Genesis)
The Evolution Conspiracy — video (Jeremiah Films)

The Fossil Record

Evolution: The Fossils Still Say No! – Duane Gish
(El Cajon, CA: Institute for Creation Research,
1995)
Stones and Bones – Wieland

Bone of Contention – Sylvia Baker (Green Forest, AR: Master Books, Inc., 1976)

Bones of Contention – Marvin Lubenow (Grand Rapids, MI: Baker Book House, Co., 1992)

In the Image of God — video (Answers in Genesis)

Evidence for a Young Earth

The Young Earth – John Morris (Green Forest, AR: Master Books, Inc., 1994)

Mount St. Helens: Explosive Evidence — Steve Austin, video (Institute for Creation Research)

Current World Issues

The Lie: Evolution – Ken Ham (Green Forest, AR: Master Books, Inc., 1987)

The Monkey Trial — Ken Ham, video lecture (Answers in Genesis)

Genesis and the Decay of the Nations – Ken Ham (Green Forest, AR: Master Books, Inc., 1991)

The Genesis Solution — Ken Ham, video (Eden Communications)

Racism

One Blood: The Biblical Answer to Racism – Ken Ham (Green Forest, AR: Master Books, Inc., 1999)

The Revised Answers Book – Batten, et al.

"Where Did the 'Races' Come From?" – Ken Ham, booklet (Answers in Genesis)

How you can be saved . . .

The Bible says there are five things you need to know about receiving eternal life.

1. Eternal life (heaven) is a gift. The Bible says: "The gift of God is eternal life through Jesus Christ our Lord" (Rom. 6:23). Like any other genuine gift, it is not earned or deserved. No amount of personal effort, good works, or religious deeds can earn a place in heaven. The Bible also states in Ephesians 2:8–9 that "By grace are ye saved through faith; and that not of yourselves: it is the gift of God: not of works, lest any man should boast." Why is it that no one can earn his or her way to heaven? That is because . . .

2. All humans are sinners — "For all have sinned, and come short of the glory of God" (Rom. 3:23). Sin is transgressing God's law and includes such things as lying, lusting, cheating, deceit, anger, evil thoughts, immoral behavior, and more. Because we are sinners, we cannot save ourselves. In fact, do you know how good you would have to be to save yourself by your own good deeds? Matthew 5:48 declares, "Be ye therefore perfect, even as your Father which is in heaven is perfect." Perfection is such a high standard that no one can save himself. However, in spite of our sin . . .

3. God is merciful. First John 4:8 says that "God is love" and in Jeremiah 31:3 He says, "I have loved thee with an everlasting love." Because God loves us, He doesn't want to punish us. God, however, is also just and therefore must punish sin. He says: "[I] will by no means clear the guilty" (Exod. 34:7) and "the soul that sinneth, it shall die" (Ezek. 18:4). We have a problem! Despite God's love for us, His justice demands that He must punish our sin. But there is a remedy . . .

4. Jesus Christ is the solution. The Bible tells us that Christ is the infinite God-Man. "In the beginning was the Word [Jesus] . . . and the Word [Jesus] was God. And the Word [Jesus] was

made flesh, and dwelt among us" (John 1:1–14). Jesus Christ — the last Adam — came to earth and lived a sinless life. He died on the Cross to pay the penalty for our sins and rose from the grave to purchase a place for us in heaven. "All we like sheep have gone astray; we have turned everyone to his own way; and the LORD hath laid on Him [Jesus] the iniquity of us all" (Isa. 53:6). Jesus Christ bore our sin in His body on the Cross and now offers you eternal life (heaven) as a gift (1 Pet. 2:24). How?

5. This gift is received by faith. Faith is the key that opens the door to heaven. Many people, however, mistake two things for saving faith:

> a. Intellectual assent, such as believing only historical facts. However, the Bible says that even the devil believes in God (James 2:19); therefore, just believing in God is not saving faith.

> b. Temporal faith, such as trusting God to solve temporary crises, including financial, family, or physical needs. While it is good to trust Christ to meet these needs, this is not saving faith.

Saving faith is trusting in Jesus Christ alone for eternal life. It means resting upon Christ alone and what He has done on the cross, rather than what you or I have done. "Believe [trust] on the Lord Jesus Christ, and thou shall be saved" (Acts 16:31).

The question that God would ask of non-believers is: Would you like to receive the gift of eternal life? You would need to transfer your trust from what you have been doing to what Christ has done for you on His cross, and then confess "with thy mouth the Lord Jesus, and shalt believe in thine heart that God hath raised Him from the dead, [and] thou shalt be saved" (Rom. 10:9).

Acts 3:19 says that you should "Repent ye therefore, and be converted, that your sins may be blotted out." Repentence is not only a heartfelt, sorrowful remorse for past sins, but also a change of mind, which is proven by a changed life. If you wish to repent, have your sins blotted out, and receive Christ as Savior, here is a suggested prayer:

> Oh, Jesus Christ, I know I am a sinner and do not deserve eternal life. But I believe You died to pay for my sins and rose from the grave to purchase a place in heaven for me. Lord Jesus, come into my life — take control of my life — forgive my sins and save me. I repent of my sins and now place my trust in You alone for my salvation. I desire to receive the free gift of eternal life.

If you have prayed this prayer of repentance, you have received the gift of eternal life! You are now a child of God — forever!

Just as a newborn baby grows physically, so now you need to grow spiritually. Read your Bible, starting perhaps with the Gospel of John, reading at least one chapter a day. Then read the first 11 chapters of the foundational Book of Genesis. Also, spend some time talking (praying) with God.

It is also important that you regularly attend a Bible-believing church that honors Christ and teaches that the Bible is the inspired Word of God and is authoritative for every aspect of your life (2 Tim. 3:15). Seek the fellowship of Christians that can help you grow in your faith. And as you grow, tell others what Christ means to you.

If you have found new life through Christ in this book, please email us at mail@answersingenesis.org or write/call one of the Answers in Genesis ministries on the following page.

Answers in Genesis International consists of the following affiliated but independent ministries.

Answers in Genesis (USA)
P.O. Box 6330
Florence, Kentucky 41022
USA

Answers in Genesis (Australia)
P.O. Box 6302
Acacia Ridge DC
QLD 4110
Australia

Answers in Genesis (Canada)
5-420 Erb St. West Suite 213
Waterloo, Ontario
Canada N2L 6K6

Answers in Genesis (NZ)
P.O. Box 39005
Howick
Auckland
New Zealand

Answers in Genesis (UK)
P.O. Box 5262
Leicester
LE2 3XU
United Kingdom

Answers in Genesis (Japan)
Attn: Nao Hanada
3317-23 Nagaoka,
Ibaraki-machi
Higashi-ibaraki-gun,
Ibaraki-ken 311-3116
Japan

For more up-to-date information on the relevance of creation and current science issues, subscribe to the full-color, quarterly magazine *Creation*.

Or . . .

For more in-depth studies, subscribe to the *Creation Ex Nihilo Technical Journal*.

Contact the AiG ministry nearest you for subscription information.

Visit our international website:
www.AnswersInGenesis.org